3-MINUTE
PRAYERS
≥for≤
BRAVE
BOYS

© 2021 by Barbour Publishing, Inc.

ISBN 978-1-64352-860-1

Published by Barbour Publishing, Inc., 1810 Barbour Drive, Uhrichsville, Ohio 44683, www.barbourbooks.com

Our mission is to inspire the world with the life-changing message of the Bible.

Member of the
Evangelical Christian
Publishers Association

Printed in the United States of America.

001217 0722 SP

3-MINUTE PRAYERS
for
BRAVE
BOYS

GLENN HASCALL

BARBOUR **kidz**

A Division of Barbour Publishing

INTRODUCTION

Never stop praying.
1 THESSALONIANS 5:17

These timely, inspiring prayers were written especially for brave boys like you!

Just three quick minutes is all you'll need to connect with your heavenly Father:

- Minute 1: Read and reflect on God's Word.
- Minute 2: Pray, using the provided prayer to jump-start a conversation with God.
- Minute 3: Reflect on a question or two for further thought.

This book isn't meant to replace your own Bible reading and study. But every one of these scriptures and prayers can help you get—and *stay!*—connected to the One who hears all your prayers. *3-Minute Prayers for Brave Boys* is a great reminder that God cares about every little and big thing you have to say. So go on—talk to Him today. God is ready and waiting to hear from you!

⇉ STAY WITH ME ⇇

*"I am the Lord your God Who holds
your right hand, and Who says to you,
'Do not be afraid. I will help you.' "*
Isaiah 41:13

Dear God, when I was smaller than I am now, I would reach out for the hand of someone bigger than me. It made me feel better. I felt safe. Sometimes I still think about holding someone's hand when I'm nervous or afraid. You want me to be brave because You know I can be brave. I don't have to be brave on my own either. I just have to hold Your hand. I don't get to see Your hand, but You care about me. When I'm scared, when I'm unsure, and when I'm overwhelmed, You stay with me and lead me to the place where You know I need to be. You will help me, so I don't need to be afraid.

BRAVE THINKING:

How does knowing that God cares
about you help you to be brave?

⧽ SIGHS ARE NO TREASURE ⧼

Lord, all my desire is before You. And my
breathing deep within is not hidden from You.
PSALM 38:9

Father, everything I have ever wanted was something You knew about. Everything I have ever needed was something You could teach me to need. I have good days, but I have bad days too. And when I sigh deep down inside and think no one knows, *You do*. I might even try to hide my struggle from other people, but I can't hide it from You. My sighs are not like a treasure I should hide. You want me to let them go, to breathe them out to You. I am brave when I let You look inside my heart and admit there are things that make me sad. I am courageous when I want to learn what You want for me. These are things I need to know.

BRAVE THINKING:

Why is it courageous to tell God
when you're having a bad day?

⋟ A BIGGER JOURNEY ⋞

*I am sure that God Who began the good
work in you will keep on working in you
until the day Jesus Christ comes again.*

PHILIPPIANS 1:6

Dear God, You've never been unemployed. When You start something, You don't give up. That means You're trustworthy. That's important to me. When I'm absolutely sure You can be trusted, I can also be brave. That's much harder to do when I'm not sure You're good. Your plans for me take me to places that seem strange and a little frightening, but those are just small stops on a bigger journey. None of those places are my forever home. You can handle anything. You *do* handle everything. Help me to be courageous enough to remember You've started something really good in my life. Help me to be brave enough to let You keep working on me.

BRAVE THINKING:

What can you do to cooperate with
the good work God is doing in you?

⇒ GOT TO CHOOSE ⇐

*You must have faith as you ask Him. You must not
doubt. Anyone who doubts is like a wave which
is pushed around by the sea. Such a man will get
nothing from the Lord. The man who has two ways
of thinking changes in everything he does.*

JAMES 1:6–8

Father, I can't expect You to help me when I
don't think You can help. Either You can help me
or You can't. I have to choose what I believe is
true. When I don't believe in You, it's like putting
a toy boat in a bathtub and hoping it will float
in the direction I want. Help me really believe
that You answer prayers. Help me trust that Your
answer is the best. Help me think the same way
about You when I tell people about You and when
I tell You what I need. Two ways of thinking keeps
me from trusting You.

BRAVE THINKING:

What's the most important thing you
need to do when you need God's help?

⋛ THE FAULT LIST ⋚

"When you say what is wrong in others, your words will be used to say what is wrong in you."

MATTHEW 7:2

God, help me to be careful with what I say about others. It's not brave to say things about people when they aren't in the same room. They can't explain what happened. I can guess. I might be wrong. I can share what I think and hurt someone else. When I keep a list of the faults of others and share them, I shouldn't be surprised when they keep a list of my faults and tell others. You know everything about me. You could tell everyone about what I did wrong. *You could.* Your list would be true. I would be hurt. People probably feel the same way when I share what I think, but I could be wrong. They would be hurt. Help me remember I'm not You, and You don't share my *sin list* with others.

BRAVE THINKING:

Why isn't it brave to say mean things about other people?

⋟ NO LONGER A STRANGER ⋞

*We can come to God without fear
because we have put our trust in Christ.*
EPHESIANS 3:12

Father, I'm glad I can be brave when I pray to You. I can be courageous when I read Your Word. I can be confident telling others about You. But there's only one way that happens—by trusting Your Son, Jesus. I can trust Jesus for rescue, forgiveness, and mercy. I can trust Him for love, kindness, and a future. When I accept all the gifts He offers, I can be brave when I talk to You. I am no longer a stranger and rebel, but I am Your child. Children should always be able to talk to a parent. I am always able to talk to You. Hearing from me is something You want. I never have to wonder if I should talk to You. *Ever.*

BRAVE THINKING:

Why would being a stranger to God
make you afraid to be near Him?

⋛ REMINDED ⋚

"Do not fear, for I am with you. Do not be afraid, for I am your God. I will give you strength, and for sure I will help you. Yes, I will hold you up with My right hand that is right and good."

ISAIAH 41:10

Dear God, sometimes I need reminders. I need to be reminded to clean my room, brush my teeth, and do my chores. I don't mean to forget, but sometimes I do. I know You want me to be brave. I know that means I don't need to be afraid. I know, but sometimes I forget. That's when I get scared, and I don't need to. So, while I'm talking to You, let me remember that You are God, You are *my* God, and You are strong when I am not. You give me strength when I have none. You help me because I need help.

BRAVE THINKING:

Why is it good to be reminded that God doesn't want you to be afraid?

⇒ FEAR IS NOT GOD'S GIFT ⇐

For God did not give us a spirit of fear.
He gave us a spirit of power and
of love and of a good mind.

2 TIMOTHY 1:7

Father, when I'm afraid, it's hard to love You and others. When I'm scared, I don't think straight—I'm confused. When I'm afraid, help me remember this was not something You want for me. Fear is not Your gift. Fear is something You don't want me to keep. You want me to be free of fear. *I need to be free of fear.* You can help me understand that I don't need fear as a friend. I can't control fear. The good news is that You are not afraid. When I give You the right to deal with my fear, You give me strength, love, and good thinking. Remove my fear. Make me strong. Make me brave.

BRAVE THINKING:

Why is it important to let
God take your fear?

⋛ IF I DON'T LET YOU TEACH ⋜

I can do all things because
Christ gives me the strength.
PHILIPPIANS 4:13

Dear God, there are things I need to learn and things I need to try. You gave me Your rules, and then You gave me the strength to follow Your rules. When I live by Your rules, You help me do things I never thought I could. You help me love others, share Your story, and discover that joy is better than happiness. The way You do things is very different from the way I do things. Your way is better. That's why I need to pay attention to You. I can't learn if I don't let You teach. I can't do anything worthwhile if You don't give me the strength to do it. Help me to be brave enough to ask You for help. Help me to be wise enough to accept Your help.

BRAVE THINKING:

Why is it important to remember
that strength comes from God?

⋛ CHOICE CHANGING ⋚

He who trusts in his own heart is a fool,
but he who walks in wisdom will be kept safe.
PROVERBS 28:26

Father, I go to school to learn things I never knew. Sometimes teachers ask me a question and I come up with an answer that's wrong. If I really knew everything, I wouldn't need to go to school. But *I don't know everything.* And if I don't know everything about math, science, and English, then I don't know everything I need to know about You. When I have questions, I can come up with the wrong answers if I'm not learning from You. There is safety in knowing the right answers—and You have them. Help me to become a courageous learner, willing student, and growing Christian. When I say something is true but I don't have the facts, I am making a foolish choice. *Teach me.*

BRAVE THINKING:

How can learning from God
change your choices?

⋚ IN CHARGE ⋚

[Jesus said,] "Peace I leave with you. My peace I give to you. I do not give peace to you as the world gives. Do not let your hearts be troubled or afraid."
JOHN 14:27

Dear God, I hear a lot about peace, and it sounds pretty good. No one fights with each other. No one disagrees. No one argues. Maybe they don't argue because they don't stand for truth. That's the peace that society wants for everyone. The problem is You say that You give a peace that's different than that. Your peace is knowing that even on days when everything seems to be going wrong, You're still in charge. When You're in charge, I don't need to be afraid. When I'm not afraid, I have peace. When I have peace, I can be brave enough to share why. This is just another one of Your amazing gifts to me—and I need peace.

BRAVE THINKING:

How is God's peace different than
the way most people think of peace?

⇒ THE OPPORTUNITY ⇐

We who have strong faith should help those who are weak. We should not live to please ourselves. Each of us should live to please his neighbor. This will help him grow in faith.

ROMANS 15:1–2

Father, You make me brave enough to help others. The more I trust You, the more You give me an opportunity to lend a hand. I could be selfish and do what I want to do, but I wouldn't be brave. I wouldn't be helpful. I wouldn't act like You. And *You want me to act like You*. Selfishness makes me weak, and it's never selfish to talk about You. Living for myself doesn't make room for You, and *You need to teach me*. I need to make room for You. When You help me grow, You give me a chance to take what I know about You and help people see how crazy awesome it would be to know You.

BRAVE THINKING:

Why does God give You opportunities
to help when you trust Him more?

⋛ BAD HABITS BOX ⋚

Put out of your life all these things: bad feelings about other people, anger, temper, loud talk, bad talk which hurts other people, and bad feelings which hurt other people.

EPHESIANS 4:31

Dear God, when I think more about me than anyone else, I can get mad pretty easily. I don't always get my way. You want me to take an imaginary box and put things inside that look a lot like jealousy and unforgiveness. When I don't *like* other people, I can't *love* them. When I get angry, I can't be kind. When I am loud, I can't listen. When I hurt their feelings, I can't be a good friend. My box of bad habits can get pretty full. I'm brave when I let You empty the box so I have room to spend time with others. Help me leave bad habits behind so nothing distracts me from taking steps in Your direction.

BRAVE THINKING:

How could filling a "bad habits box" make it easier to follow God?

WALK TOWARD GOD TOGETHER

Comfort those who feel they cannot keep going on. Help the weak. Understand and be willing to wait for all men.

1 THESSALONIANS 5:14

Father, I know people who struggle. I've had hard days too. I don't want to make their lives harder. Help me to be a friend to those who need a reason to keep going. So many people want to give up. You don't give them a reason to do that, and neither should I. You help me when I'm weak. Would You give me the words to encourage those who are uncertain? Some people will have trouble taking the next step. Help me remember what that's like and be willing to wait for them so we can walk toward You together. You walk with me, encourage me, and help me every moment of every day. I want that for everyone I know.

BRAVE THINKING:

How does helping those who are weak remind you of Jesus?

⋛ LOVE AND RESPECT ⋚

Love each other as Christian brothers.
Show respect for each other.
ROMANS 12:10

Dear God, when I love other people, I'm making a choice. When I show respect for other people, it's also a choice. Both choices mean I'm willing to obey You. That's a brave choice because many people don't choose to love or respect. But it's easy to be brave when I'm obeying You. The plans You have are good, Your love is overwhelming, and I can be confident knowing that You bring good to those who choose to love You. I have an example to follow, and Your example is love. Your command is to respect. When I think I'm better than other people, I can't show love or respect. You showed both to people who were guilty of breaking Your laws. You did what only You could do and then offered to help me do the same.

BRAVE THINKING:

Why is it important for you
to love and respect others?

⇒ GOD'S BETTER OPTIONS ⇐

*The man who shows loving-kindness does himself
good, but the man without pity hurts himself.*
Proverbs 11:17

Father, I could make choices that help me but
hurt others. I could think about myself and
ignore people You love. I could even choose
selfishness over kindness. And I would only be
hurting myself. How do I know this is true? You
told me in Your Word. I could listen to others. I
could be sad when they're sad. I could do something to help them. *I could.* It's easy to think that
loving-kindness is something only You give,
but it's something You also ask me to share. I
wouldn't know how if it weren't for You. I don't
want to hurt others by being selfish. You have
better options—love and kindness. Let those be
my choices.

BRAVE THINKING:

How can love and kindness
make you a better friend?

⋛ BEYOND STRUGGLE ⋚

*We are glad for our troubles also. We know
that troubles help us learn not to give up.*
ROMANS 5:3

Dear God, I don't like to struggle. Hard times are not my idea of a good day. I'd like to live without trouble. But You say there is a purpose for my problems, wisdom for my worry, and delight after my distress. When I have to go through something I would rather avoid, You can help me learn something. And what I learn helps me and can help others. When I survive the difficult, it's a step of bravery. You want me to endure struggle because it helps me understand that everyone struggles, and their struggles are real. When I move beyond struggle, I can encourage others to move beyond theirs. Thank You for encouraging me never to give up.

BRAVE THINKING:

How can struggles play a positive
part in growing with Jesus?

⋛ BEGGING FOR ATTENTION? ⋚

[Jesus said,] "Whoever makes himself look more important than he is will find out how little he is worth. Whoever does not try to honor himself will be made important."

LUKE 14:11

Father, I want to be good at something. You want me to be successful at something. But what You want me to be good at may not be what I think I'm good at. You can teach me. I will get impatient. I might try to prove to other people that I'm the best at something, but that's not being brave; it's begging for attention. You already pay attention to me. Help me pay attention to what You're teaching. And if I become good at what You've made me to do, then I can honor You and You can use me to do something You know I can do.

BRAVE THINKING:

Why is it important to be good at what God made you to do?

≳ I AM UNDONE ≲

The Holy Spirit helps us where we are weak.
We do not know how to pray or what we should
pray for, but the Holy Spirit prays to God for us.
ROMANS 8:26

Dear God, I don't have all the answers. I don't say all the right words. I'm weaker than I want to be. *You aren't surprised.* You have all the answers. You know all the right words. You're stronger than I'll ever be. Your Spirit helps me meet with You when I am speechless, when I am scared, and when I can't even think of what to say. When Your Spirit helps me, I am confident. I don't deserve Your help. I didn't expect You to notice me. But I'm here. You help me. I am noticed. I am Your child. Let's keep talking.

BRAVE THINKING:

How does it help knowing that
God's Spirit can help you pray?

⋝ THE ONE WHO IS STRONGER ⋜

You answered me on the day I called.
You gave me strength in my soul.
PSALM 138:3

Father, not every day is memorable. Not every moment is happy. Not every decision is wise. I can feel lost and alone. When I'm in trouble or cause trouble or trouble finds me, help me remember to call Your name and ask for help. You answer, and You *have* answers. You're strong, and You give me strength. I call, and You care about me. You give me a reason to be brave. If I keep close to the only One who is stronger than anyone or anything else, then the only explanation is that You make me strong. You strengthen my character and my ability to make good choices, and You make my heart strong when I am frightened. When I call, *You answer*. When You answer, *I grow strong*.

BRAVE THINKING:

How is it possible to gain strength
by asking God for help?

⋛ ROOTS RUN DEEP ⋚

Have your roots planted deep in Christ. Grow in Him. Get your strength from Him. Let Him make you strong in the faith as you have been taught. Your life should be full of thanks to Him.

COLOSSIANS 2:7

Dear God, if I pull a dandelion, I'm likely to leave some of the root in the ground. The roots are really long. They go down deep. The dandelion can't grow without the root. You want me to have deep roots that link my life on earth with my relationship with Your Son, Jesus. When those roots go deep, I can't help but grow and become strong and become hard to pull up if something threatens to uproot me. Help me grow strong again. When I trust You, it's that trust that gives me courage never to stop growing.

BRAVE THINKING:

Why is it important to think of your Christian life as having roots?

⋛ CHANGED AND REARRANGED ⋚

All the Holy Writings are God-given and are made alive by Him. Man is helped when he is taught God's Word. It shows what is wrong. It changes the way of a man's life. It shows him how to be right with God.
2 TIMOTHY 3:16

Father, if I write down my thoughts, I will probably forget what I wrote in a week. I might change my mind. I might learn more and realize that what I originally thought was wrong. Your words can show me a better way. Your words live in hearts and minds. They change choices. They rearrange futures. They make relationships grow. Help me when I read them. Teach me when I know them. Invite me to come close to You when I understand what You've said. How can I be fearful when You've written the words? You don't forget. You don't change Your mind.

BRAVE THINKING:

How can you be more confident by
reading God's words in the Bible?

⋛ NEVER TOO BUSY ⋚

*Jesus called the followers to Him and
said, "Let the little children come
to Me. Do not try to stop them."*
LUKE 18:16

Dear God, You never stop me from spending time with You. You don't want anyone else to stop me from spending time with you either. Jesus' disciples probably thought they were doing a good thing by keeping kids away from Him. But Jesus gave kids a reason to be brave. He told His disciples to step out of the way because He wanted to talk to kids just like me. He wanted to listen. He wanted to spend time with them. Jesus wasn't too busy or too important to notice kids and teach them. Jesus loves children. He loves adults. He loves everyone. And the best news is that Jesus never keeps anyone from talking to Him.

BRAVE THINKING:

Why is it important to know that Jesus didn't want to stop kids from spending time with Him?

⇒ CHOSEN AND USEFUL ⇐

*[God] gives us everything we need for life and
for holy living. He gives it through His great power.*
2 PETER 1:3

Father, You make sure that I get everything I need. I may never be rich, but I can be satisfied. You made life to be like that. You make sure that I get everything I need to be set apart as someone chosen to do what You need done. I may never seem important, but I can be helpful. You made holiness to be like that. You send what I need, and You're strong enough to make sure these gifts are delivered on time. You're strong enough to take care of me when things seem bad. You're strong enough to make someone like me useful. *You have always been strong enough.* Make me wise enough to notice and accept what You offer.

BRAVE THINKING:

Why is it important that God pays more
attention to your needs than your wish list?

⋦ KEEP READING ⋧

*We must listen all the more to the
truths we have been told. If we do not,
we may slip away from them.*

HEBREWS 2:1

Dear God, when I was told to share my toys, I didn't want to, but I obeyed. I wasn't sure it was a good idea, but I noticed that other kids shared more when I shared. Every time I listened to that voice telling me to share, I was learning that it was important to share. I'm still learning. When You tell me the right choices to make, I learn more every time I'm reminded. When I stop reading Your Word, the less I remember. I could even forget when I stay away too long. Reading the Bible means I am learning. When I learn from You, I become courageous.

BRAVE THINKING:

Why can it become easy to forget
what You learned from God?

⤜ A GOOD OUTCOME ⤛

Be happy in your hope. Do not give up when trouble comes. Do not let anything stop you from praying.
ROMANS 12:12

Father, when I run, I don't stop when I stumble. I get up and keep going. When I struggle with homework, I don't give up when I want to learn. When the next bad day comes, You don't want me to stop trusting, believing, and hoping. When I hope in You, it's more than just thinking You might help me if no one else does. Hope trusts. Hope believes. Hope is being sure that You have a good outcome for me each time trouble shows up. So today I pray. The words come from my heart to Your ear. And I don't want to stop this conversation with You. I am satisfied because You love me. I am strong because You make me brave. I pray because talking to You helps me hold on.

BRAVE THINKING:

Why does God use hope to describe
His preferred way to trust Him?

⋛ WILLING STUDENT ⋚

[God] leads those without pride into
what is right, and teaches them His way.
PSALM 25:9

Dear God, I'm wrong when I think I'm smarter than You. I know that doesn't surprise You. If I know everything, then there is no reason for You to teach me. When I'm honest and admit I need You to teach me, You *will* teach me. When I try to learn on my own, the best I can do is learn something from my mistakes. If I learn from You, I don't need to make so many mistakes. You want me to be a willing student. I can't be that kind of student if I don't think You have anything I need to learn or think that You just don't understand what it's like to be a boy today. Help me understand the way You want me to live.

BRAVE THINKING:

When learning from God, what kind
of student do you want to be?

⋛ TEAMWORK ⋛

We are His work. He has made us to belong
to Christ Jesus so we can work for Him.
He planned that we should do this.

Ephesians 2:10

Father, when I think about football, baseball, or basketball, I think about teams and the people who play on those teams. Some teams I like. I'm a fan. I might wear a shirt or hat with a team name. I might even know how many games they've won or what team they will play next. Christians are part of Your team. Do I know as much about You? I am part of Your team. Help me learn to work with my teammates. You created this team. You know we will win, but there are plenty of games to play, and there's only one real rival. You have a game plan. Help me follow it. Help me endure. Help my team.

BRAVE THINKING:

How can it help to think of the Christian
life as being part of God's team?

⋛ THE NARROW PLACE ⋛

We are pressed on every side, but we still have room to move. We are often in much trouble, but we never give up. People make it hard for us, but we are not left alone. We are knocked down, but we are not destroyed.
2 CORINTHIANS 4:8–9

Dear God, You say that the Christian walk is like a narrow path. Maybe that's because trouble pushes in from the sides, leaving me a very narrow place to walk. You tell me I will always have room to move in Your direction. Because I know You give me room to move, I don't give up in the middle of struggles. You walk with me, and I'm never alone. When I get pushed down, You pick me up and I realize You never allow me to be destroyed. Each setback leads me to bravely walk Your path forward.

BRAVE THINKING:

How does it help to know that
God has a direction for you?

⋛ SEND FEAR AWAY ⋚

"Have I not told you? Be strong and have strength of heart! Do not be afraid or lose faith. For the Lord your God is with you anywhere you go."

JOSHUA 1:9

Father, when I'm alone, I can think things that make me afraid. When school starts, I can be afraid because I don't know everyone in my class. I can be afraid that I will get lost, meet a bully, or struggle. Joshua could have been speaking to me when he said, "Be strong and have strength of heart!" He must have known how I felt when he said, "Do not be afraid or lose faith." He knew I needed to remember, "The Lord your God is with you anywhere you go." Your Word makes me brave because it gives me the words I need to read, know, and remember. They encourage me. They send fear away.

BRAVE THINKING:

Why do you think fear weakens your ability to trust God?

⇝ THE THINGS GOD DOES ⇜

We know we are not able in ourselves to do any of this work. God makes us able to do these things.

2 CORINTHIANS 3:5

Dear God, You don't want me to trust myself—*You want me to trust You.* I need to remember I can't do any good thing on my own. I will always need Your help. You say my heart is deceitful. My feelings can lie to me. It sounds like I'm weak, and if I'm weak, then how can I be brave? You make me that way. You fill me with Your strength, and my weakness goes away. You give me something to do and then help me do it. This kind of bravery means I don't pretend to do something only You can do, I don't start a journey without You by my side, and I don't take credit for the things You do. *I accept your help.*

BRAVE THINKING:

How has your idea of bravery changed
while praying these prayers?

⋛ FOR MY GOOD ⋚

"The Lord your God is with you, a Powerful
One Who wins the battle. He will have much joy
over you. With His love He will give you new life.
He will have joy over you with loud singing."

ZEPHANIAH 3:17

Father, You are with me. You never leave me. You are mighty. You win battles. You lead me. You watch where I go. You've given me a new life, and You want to watch me grow. I could call you "Mighty to Save" or "With Me Forever" or even "The God Who Loves Me." When I'm around You, I realize that You have great power and You want to use it for my good. I can be brave because I don't have to be afraid. I don't have to be afraid because I am loved. I am loved because You made me to be loved.

BRAVE THINKING:

How does the thought of God
loving you make you less fearful?

⋛ SOUNDS LIKE THE TRUTH ⋚

*The time will come when people will not
listen to the truth. They will look for teachers
who will tell them only what they want to
hear. They will not listen to the truth. Instead,
they will listen to stories made up by men.*
2 TIMOTHY 4:3–4

Dear God, I want to know the truth, but I have listened to lies and have even believed things that weren't true. Sometimes when people tell a lie over and over again, it can sound like the truth. Telling a lie is not courageous. Lies don't deserve applause, medals, or parades. I've heard that some people hate Your truth so much they will tell lies about You. They will look for other people who will lie about You too. When I need to know the truth, help me come to You for answers.

BRAVE THINKING:

Why is it easy to believe a lie
even when you know the truth?

ϟ A WORK BEGUN ϟ

I am sure that God Who began the good
work in you will keep on working in you
until the day Jesus Christ comes again.

PHILIPPIANS 1:6

Father, I can start a puzzle and never finish it. I can take lessons on playing an instrument and then quit. I can even say I'll try a new food and refuse to taste it. That's me, but it's not You. If I'm a puzzle, You don't stop until the last piece is in place. *You don't stop.* You started work on me, and You keep looking for times when You can teach me, move me, and make me into the person You had in mind all along. You started this new life living. You keep working on me. You plan to finish what You started. I can gain confidence when I see the change You're making in me.

BRAVE THINKING:

Why should you want God to keep working to grow you into the man He wants you to be?

≳ THE HELP I NEED ≲

Do not let sin have power over you.
Let good have power over sin!
ROMANS 12:21

Dear God, sometimes I think I can't stop making bad choices. You call it sin, and it means I break Your rules. You say that everyone sins. *Everyone.* If this is a competition, then I will always lose. But You want me to win. You want me to say no to sin. You offer the help I need. I can let sin become powerful or remember that You're more powerful than sin. I can let sin win, or I can watch You win. I can give up and make wrong choices, or I can give You the chance to help me make right choices. I don't want sin to be my first choice. I want You to rescue me the next time I think of doing something I know breaks Your rules and makes You sad.

BRAVE THINKING:

What can you do when you think it might be a good idea to break God's rules?

⋛ IMPRESSED AND LOVED ⋛

[Jesus said,] "If you love Me,
you will do what I say."
JOHN 14:15

Father, I say that I love You. I think I mean it. I've heard the stories. I've read about Your love for me. You have always impressed me, God. You don't ask me to prove my love for You, but You've told me how I can tell that I do love You: *when I do what You say.* That's when I'm brave. That's when I trust You enough to believe in Your good plan. That's when I'm strong enough to follow even if few people seem to follow. That's when I'm confident enough to take Your hand and let You lead me. I say that I love You, and I can know when I mean it—the only thing I need is the choice to obey.

BRAVE THINKING:

Why is obedience the best way
to know that you love God?

⋛ UNDEFEATABLE ⋜

*The One Who lives in you is stronger
than the one who is in the world.*

1 JOHN 4:4

Dear God, I don't always understand everything about You, but I want to. You say You live in my life, but I don't know how that happens. I do know that You can help me when I don't know what to do next. You help me when I have questions. *You help me.* And because You're strong, because You live in me, and because You love me, I don't have to be afraid. I'm strong because You're with me. There is no one stronger than You. No one wins an argument with You. No one can defeat You. *You are God.* No one compares to You. When Your enemy tries to convince me that he's stronger, help me remember he's only good at telling lies. You are stronger. You have truth. I want to understand. Help me.

BRAVE THINKING:

How is it possible to live without fear?

⇝ WHEN MY HOPE IS IN YOU ⇜

*Our hope comes from God. May He fill you with joy
and peace because of your trust in Him. May your
hope grow stronger by the power of the Holy Spirit.*
ROMANS 15:13

Father, when I say my hope is in You, it means
I know beyond any doubt that You have *every-thing* worked out. The hope You give me doesn't
give doubt a spare room. Hope trusts when it
would be easier to be cautious, believes when
it would be easier to reject, and grips faith when
it would be easier to go my own way. When I
have hope, I also have joy and peace. My hope
grows stronger because You're with me. And
when my hope is in You and from You, I can
be confident that Your strength can make me
braver than I think I can be.

BRAVE THINKING:

Why can't hope and doubt work
together when you follow Jesus?

⋛ FOR YOU ⋚

Since God is for us, who can be against us?
ROMANS 8:31

Dear God, when a friend turns his back and doesn't treat me like a friend, help me remember that You are for me. When a bully is mean and laughs at me, help me remember that You never leave me. When someone says something unkind about me, help me remember that You love me. What You think matters more than the rejection of friends, the laughter of bullies, and the unkindness of strangers. Because You are for me, the opinions of other people will always mean less than Your opinion of me. When people are against me but You are for me, Your opinion will always be the most important. I will never be alone when people speak words that hurt. You've heard mean words too. It's good to know You understand.

BRAVE THINKING:

Why can it seem that the voices of people who are against you seem louder than God's reminder that He has never been against you?

⋛ WHAT YOU DID FOR ME ⋚

You must be kind to each other. Think of the other person. Forgive other people just as God forgave you because of Christ's death on the cross.

EPHESIANS 4:32

Father, it's easy to think about me because I know me more than most. I know what I like, what I want, and what will make me happy. You want me to think about other people. You want me to be kind to them. You want me to forgive them when they do something wrong. And if I ever wanted to know why I should do these things, You gave me the answer. I offer something that other people don't deserve because that's what You did for me. Jesus did all these things when He died on the cross for people who were unkind and selfish and refused to forgive. He did what they would not do.

BRAVE THINKING:

Why is it important that Jesus shows you how to be kind and how to forgive?

⫷ NOTHING IS WASTED ⫸

Be strong. Do not allow anyone to change your mind.
Always do your work well for the Lord. You know
that whatever you do for Him will not be wasted.
1 Corinthians 15:58

Dear God, when You tell me to be strong, it's because I should already be trusting You. You tell me not to let anyone change my mind. That's because You've already changed mine. I don't need to go back to old thinking. You tell me to do my work well for You. That's because You have some really good things for me to do and people will notice how I do things. There are all kinds of things that can waste my time. When I do things for You, nothing is wasted. *Nothing.* So today I will be brave because You can make me strong. I will serve You. Help me serve well.

BRAVE THINKING:

When is the right time to be brave? Why?

⋛ MORE IMPORTANT THAN ⋚

*"Do not work for food that does not last.
Work for food that lasts forever. The Son
of Man will give you that kind of food."*
JOHN 6:27

Father, since You can be trusted to give me what
I need, I can work for You without worrying about
those things. I can work on things more important than food or clothing. I can offer my help
on things that are important to You. Food has an
expiration date, and clothes change styles. What
You do lasts forever. I can be hungry to learn. You
can make sure I am full when I read Your words
in Your Book. I can spend a lot of time thinking about what I need, but You already do that.
Maybe I should spend more time learning what's
important to You.

BRAVE THINKING:

How can it help you to let God
take care of what you need?

⋛ YOU HELP ME ⋚

[Jesus answered Paul,] "I am all you need.
I give you My loving-favor. My power works
best in weak people." I am happy to be weak and
have troubles so I can have Christ's power in me.
2 CORINTHIANS 12:9

Dear God, I'm weak. You're strong. But You never treat me like I'm worthless. I'm used to seeing people that look strong act like I don't have value. When I say I'm weak, You don't laugh at me; You help me. Maybe You like to help people who refuse to act like they can do everything on their own. When I figure out that You can do what I can't, that's when You step in and help me most. You are all I need. You're kind. You love me. So when I feel weak and the headlines of my day read TROUBLE, help me.

BRAVE THINKING:

What are the benefits of being weak?

⤜ CRUSHED AND BROKEN ⤛

The Lord is near to those who have a broken heart.
And He saves those who are broken in spirit.
PSALM 34:18

Father, some people think that when others say or do mean things to me, I should just bounce back. That's harder than it sounds when I'm sad and feel alone. It's almost like they are asking me to forget that something bad happened. On my own? I can't do that. I remember the mean words. I remember the way I felt when they were said. I don't want to keep feeling that way. It's good to know that I don't have to. You show up when I feel crushed and broken. I don't live in a perfect world, and sometimes bad things happen to people who don't deserve it. I don't want to get even. I don't want to get ahead. I want to walk with You and learn about Your kindness, forgiveness, and love.

BRAVE THINKING:

Why is it important that God is
really close on the bad days?

⇒ LET'S TALK ⇐

Dear God, when I'm encouraged to do the wrong thing, I will sometimes *do* the wrong thing. When I know the right choice, sometimes I won't get the job done. When I let You down, I want to hide, but that's not what You want me to do. You want me to come talk to You and not be shy. Jesus was encouraged to do the wrong thing too. He understands. The difference between me and Jesus is that I've done the wrong thing but He never did. I'm comfortable knowing that when I talk to You and You forgive me, You give me love, kindness, and favor and help me make much better choices.

BRAVE THINKING:

Why can you be brave when talking to God about what you've done wrong?

⋛ THE CLEAR PATH ⋚

Trust in the Lord with all your heart, and do not trust in your own understanding. Agree with Him in all your ways, and He will make your paths straight.

PROVERBS 3:5–6

Father, if I want Your best for my life, then I need to follow Your plan, not mine. When I trust me more than You, I'm failing the class. When I want the ability to choose my own path, I'm not following Yours. When I recognize Your direction but spend time wondering what I'm missing by following only Your path, I'm doubting You and trusting myself more. There is nothing about You that can't be trusted. You make the path straight so it's easier to follow. And when I agree that You are trustworthy and have given me a clear path, that's when I can go places—with You.

BRAVE THINKING:

How can following your own plan
leave you without courage?

⸙ LEARN THE REASONS ⸘

*A man's understanding makes him
slow to anger. It is to his honor to forgive
and forget a wrong done to him.*
PROVERBS 19:11

Dear God, I get to learn new things every day.
Sometimes I learn science or history. Sometimes
I'm a student of other people. That's why I need
to know You. When I know You, I can learn how
to treat other people. I can also learn the reasons why people act the way they do. When I
have Your help in understanding people, I don't
get angry with them as much and I can love them
more. You consider me a boy worth honoring
when I forgive people when they mistreat me.
When I forgive them, it shows that I am learning from You and understanding the people You
have created. Understanding others starts with
understanding You.

BRAVE THINKING:

Why is it so hard to understand other people?

⋛ THE CROOKED COURSE ⋚

It is not good for a person to be
without much learning, and he who
hurries with his feet rushes into sin.

<small>PROVERBS 19:2</small>

Father, not all learning happens in a school building. You can teach me anywhere, and *I need to learn from You*. It's not good for me to stop learning. It's not right for me to refuse to start. When I guess what I should do, I'm on a crooked course away from You and on a shortcut to sin. It's easy to get off track. *I have gotten off track*. You can help me leave this place for Your side. Help me move beyond reading Your words to understanding and obeying them. Help me choose Your side over any promises of something better. Those kinds of promises are always broken. It must make You very sad when I say I want to follow You and then walk away. I don't want to make You sad.

BRAVE THINKING:

When it comes to following God,
how can you stay on track?

⋛ THE JOURNEY ⋛

Turn away from the sinful things young people want to do. Go after what is right. Have a desire for faith and love and peace. Do this with those who pray to God from a clean heart.
2 TIMOTHY 2:22

Dear God, if I ever want to play follow the leader, then I want You to be my leader. I can get into trouble by myself. I can also get into trouble when I do things friends ask me to do. Help me choose the right thing over mistakes. Help me choose faith over fear, love over hate, and peace over conflict. Help me to ask others who want the same things to join me. We can travel together on this journey with You. I can be brave knowing that You are for me and that I have friends with me.

BRAVE THINKING:

How can good friends encourage you to follow God?

⋛ GET TO KNOW YOU ⋚

I looked for the Lord, and He answered me.
And He took away all my fears.

PSALM 34:4

Father, some people think You're scary. It's probably because they've never really met You. People should get to know You because You want to be known. You don't make it hard to find You. When I pray, I find answers in Your Word. You ask people to open their eyes, hearts, and minds and really look. Every time I do, I discover You. I discover Your plan. I discover that this faith growing in me is making less room for fear. You made everything, and You can do anything. Some people think that because You're so powerful, You're just looking for a moment when You can hurt people. But Your Word says that You love to show mercy. You created people to love and have fellowship with them. So I'll keep looking for You, You'll keep answering, and I'll watch fear go away.

BRAVE THINKING:

Why does fear go away when you get to know God?

⋛ NOT FAKE ⋚

Some are weak. I have become weak so I might lead them to Christ. I have become like every person so in every way I might lead some to Christ.

1 CORINTHIANS 9:22

Dear God, You want me to understand other people. When I understand them, I have a better idea of how to tell them about You. If they struggle, it's easy to remember what that feels like, and I can tell them about how You help when I struggle. This is why it was so important that Jesus came to earth to see what it's like to be human. When He learned what it was like, He could help a kid like me understand Him more. Jesus became a human to help humans understand how to become His friends. I get to help others see Jesus just by being real and truthful about my own struggles and telling them how You help me.

BRAVE THINKING:

Why can't bravery and pretending exist together when telling other people about Jesus?

⋧ STAND IN HOPE ⋦

*When we have learned not to give up,
it shows we have stood the test. When
we have stood the test, it gives us hope.*

ROMANS 5:4

Father, some people run a race just to prove to themselves they can do it. When they finish a short race, they might even want to try a longer race the next time. They call this type of courage *endurance*. When someone finishes a test, they are a little closer to finishing a class. They spend a lot of time studying and memorizing so that when that final test comes, it is much easier to get through. You teach me not to give up. You teach me not to avoid tests. You teach me to stand up, stand strong, and stand hopeful. So today *I stand*. You give courage as a gift every time I take a step with You.

BRAVE THINKING:

Why is it important to endure tests?

⋛ BAD IDEAS OUT ⋚

*A man who cannot rule his own spirit is
like a city whose walls are broken down.*
PROVERBS 25:28

Dear God, if a city has walls, then the people who live in that city expect protection from the walls. Those walls can protect against enemies, provide safety, and act as a boundary for all to see. When even a small bit of the wall is broken, anyone can come in. Anyone can bring danger to the people of the city. Anyone can ignore the boundaries. This is what happens in my life when I choose to ignore what I know I should do. It's like the wall that protects my heart is broken and bad ideas walk through without being stopped. Those ideas can cause problems just like a broken city wall. Keep the bad ideas out. Keep the good ideas in a protected mind and heart. That's what You can do for me.

BRAVE THINKING:

Why is it important to keep your
mind and heart protected?

⋝ WORDS EXPRESSED ⋜

God's Word is living and powerful. It is sharper
than a sword that cuts both ways. It cuts straight
into where the soul and spirit meet and it divides
them. . . . It tells what the heart is thinking
about and what it wants to do.

HEBREWS 4:12

Father, You wrote words that bring life and display Your power. Those words are to the point, have a point, and point to You. If these words were a knife, they could be used to remove any sin I've let grow in my life. Please heal me. These words express who You are. If Your words are sharper than a sword with edges on both sides, then I need to remember that this sword was never meant to be used to hurt others but to bring clear wisdom to hard issues. When I use the Bible as this kind of sword, I bravely learn from You.

BRAVE THINKING:

Do you know some benefits of
reading the Bible? Name a few.

⇒ GOOD AND FAIR ⇐

*Good will come to the man who is ready
to give much, and fair in what he does. . . .
He will not be afraid of bad news. His heart
is strong because he trusts in the Lord.*
PSALM 112:5, 7

Dear God, looking out for other people is a sign of strength and bravery. You are brave all the time, and You reward this kind of bravery. When I give to others and treat them fairly, You deliver good wherever I'm at. *You're never late.* When I am this brave, You say I don't need to be afraid when I hear bad news. This type of bravery means that I trust You and believe You will help and that I'm confident in the outcome. Give me hands willing to help, a heart willing to love, and a mind that makes fair decisions.

BRAVE THINKING:

Why are some of God's blessings
linked to your decisions?

THE BRAVE WERE ONCE AFRAID

The Lord is my light and the One Who saves me.
Whom should I fear? The Lord is the strength of
my life. Of whom should I be afraid? ... Even if an
army gathers against me, my heart will not be afraid.
Even if war rises against me, I will be sure of You.
PSALM 27:1, 3

Father, when I'm afraid of the dark, You're my light. When I need to be rescued, You save me. When I need a place to feel safe, You make sure I have immediate access to You. When I feel like I'm in the middle of a battle, You make me brave. I am learning that brave people were once afraid but discovered that You can help them face their fears. There is nothing so big that You worry about it. If You don't worry about my fears, then it makes sense that I shouldn't either. After all, You are my Light, my Rescuer, and my Safe Place, and You make me brave.

BRAVE THINKING:

How can you be brave knowing
that God does not worry?

DON'T THROW AWAY WHAT YOU SHOULD KEEP

Do not throw away your trust,
for your reward will be great.
HEBREWS 10:35

Dear God, if I were asked what I could throw away, I could come up with a list. I'd be willing to throw away old fast-food bags, used paper cups, and an unused box. Throwing these things away wouldn't be much of a loss. I wouldn't miss the bag, the cups, or the box. Some things, like a special gift from a friend, I would never throw away. Some things, like an old worn-out sweatshirt or bad decision-making, I'm hesitant to throw away but should. And there is something You don't want me to throw away: trust. Trust is what allows me to believe in You. Trust is the best friend of faith. Trust keeps company with hope. When I trust You, I accept adventure. Be my guide.

BRAVE THINKING:

Why is trusting God something He rewards?

THE PROBLEM WITH TWO OPINIONS

"No one can have two bosses. He will hate the one and love the other. Or he will listen to the one and work against the other. You cannot have both God and riches as your boss at the same time."

MATTHEW 6:24

Father, You want to teach me. You want to show me the right things to do, and You want me to follow You. That's a good thing for me to remember, because when I forget, I follow people instead. I can follow You, or I can follow someone else. I can't do both. I can't be loyal to two different opinions. I can't follow You and make something else more important than You. I can't be brave if I don't follow You. Help me point my will in Your direction.

BRAVE THINKING:

Why is being loyal to God a sign of courage?

⋛ STRONGER ⋚

[God] gives strength to the weak. And He
gives power to him who has little strength.
ISAIAH 40:29

Dear God, when I'm sick I get weak. I have to eat a few good meals before I feel stronger. Regular meals keep my body as strong as possible. Someone once called the Bible "daily bread." When I read Your words, it's like feeding my soul. It gives me strength when I am weak. I don't have to live with just a little strength. On my own I am weak, and I only get weaker without You. But when I need strength and when I want to be brave, then I need You. Please take a weak spirit and give me strength. Take a weak mind and replace it with strong wisdom. Take a weak will and make me brave. I don't know why You trade me Your best for my worst, but I am thankful.

BRAVE THINKING:

How can God's strength replace your weakness?

⇥ GRATEFUL ⇤

*"O give thanks to the Lord, for He is good.
His loving-kindness lasts forever."*
1 CHRONICLES 16:34

Father, You are good and I'm grateful. You are the kind of good that knows what's best, does what's right, and shares what I could never buy. You are good when I'm not. You do good even when I won't. You're good even when I'm not searching. In Your goodness, You chased someone like me: a rule breaker, rebel, and promise breaker. I can't do what You do, but I can let You do what You know is best in my life and the lives of others. I don't want to stop You, interrupt, or stand in Your way. Your love doesn't stop when I prove I can't be trusted. Your love is never put on hold. Your love lasts forever. You're good. You love me. That's awesome.

BRAVE THINKING:

When is the best time to be
grateful to God? Why?

NOT EMBARRASSED— NOT ASHAMED

Do your best to know that God is pleased with you. Be as a workman who has nothing to be ashamed of.

2 TIMOTHY 2:15

Dear God, when I want You to be pleased with me, I just need to remember to do what You want me to do. If I work for You, I need to do everything I can to please You. I want to do my work well enough that I don't have to be embarrassed or ashamed. I can be confident reading Your Word, knowing Your Word, and sharing Your Word because this is what pleases You. It is this kind of work that I never need to be ashamed of doing. You don't want me to be ashamed. You want to be pleased with my choice to share You with others.

BRAVE THINKING:

Why should you want to please God?

⋛ KEEP RUNNING ⋚

*I run straight for the place at the
end of the race. I fight to win.*

1 CORINTHIANS 9:26

Father, some races are meant to be run fast—the runner starts and ends fast. Some races are finished by endurance runners who may not start as fast, but they set a pace that helps them finish sooner than other runners. The race You want me to run starts with You and ends with You. The pace is less important than the finish. I'm not racing against others; I'm just running with You because the finish line is amazing. Endurance makes me brave. The longer I walk with You, the more I believe I can finish this race. The more You run with me, the more I believe You will run with me. The more You encourage me, the more encouraged I am. This is the race You made for me. Help me to be strong enough never to give up.

BRAVE THINKING:

Why is it important that
God is with you in the race?

WHERE I DON'T WANT TO WALK

Yes, even if I walk through the valley of the shadow of death, I will not be afraid of anything, because You are with me. You have a walking stick with which to guide and one with which to help. These comfort me.

PSALM 23:4

Dear God, there are places I don't want to walk. Maybe the traffic is bad, maybe it's nighttime in a dark place, or maybe I've never been in that place before. I get uncomfortable, nervous, or very afraid, and I don't want to walk in these places *unless someone is with me*. But when I realize that You are always with me, I am no longer afraid. When I can't see where to go, You lead me. When I am uncomfortable, You comfort me. That's what You do because that's who You are.

BRAVE THINKING:

Why is it so easy to be afraid of things that you don't understand?

⋛ CARE ABOUT EVERYONE ⋜

You must pray at all times as the Holy Spirit leads you to pray. Pray for the things that are needed. You must watch and keep on praying. Remember to pray for all Christians.

EPHESIANS 6:18

Father, there's never a bad time to pray. When I'm sad, happy, or thinking about doing something I know You don't want me to do, I should pray. Talking to You shouldn't be something I try to get out of—I should want to pray. Your Spirit might convince me it's time to talk. I don't need a special reason; I just need a chance to speak and a willingness to listen. You want me to pray for things needed. That could be for my family, friends, neighbors, or someone I heard about on the news. I should pray for Christians. It's not very brave to think only about my needs. Help me remember that You care about everyone.

BRAVE THINKING:

Why is it brave to care about everyone?

WEAK. WEARY. DESPERATE. NEEDY.

My body and my heart may grow weak,
but God is the strength of my heart
and all I need forever.

PSALM 73:26

Dear God, You said You would take care of all my needs. Turns out, You already have, because all I really need is You. And I don't just need You today or tomorrow. I didn't even *just* need you yesterday or last year. I need You now. I need You forever. You bring me gifts of hope when I'm hurting. You bring strength to my heart when it seems weak. When I get weak and feel weary or when I have a need and feel desperate, I can be courageous because You are the remedy for weakness and the answer to need. Nothing I do on my own will ever outdo what You can do. Please, do that for me.

BRAVE THINKING:

When do you need Jesus? Why?

⇌ STOP LOOKING BACK ⇌

*I do one thing. I forget everything
that is behind me and look forward
to that which is ahead of me.*

PHILIPPIANS 3:13

Father, I've made mistakes and I've broken Your law. *I have sinned.* Accepting Your forgiveness and forgetting the past should be easy. *But I can't.* When I think about the past, I think two different thoughts. The first is that if I could go back, I would want to make a better choice. The other thought is that I might want to make the same mistake. What's wrong with me? You want me to look ahead and not behind. You want me to forget the past and remember that You have a future planned for me that will need my attention. *I need Your help.* I can't pay attention to where You're taking me if I'm always looking behind me to where I've been.

BRAVE THINKING:

Why is looking forward instead
of looking back a brave choice?

⋛ THE TROUBLE RUN ⋚

The sinful run away when no one is trying to catch them, but those who are right with God have as much strength of heart as a lion.
PROVERBS 28:1

Dear God, I can run from trouble. It's easy but not always helpful. Trouble finds me no matter where I go. But You don't want me to run, jog, or even walk away from You. When I'm in trouble, I should run as fast as I can *to* You. The further I run away from You, the weaker I get. It's a foolish thing to think You would hate me because I sin. It must make You very sad when I think that way. When I make the bold choice to walk with You and do what You say, I become strong. When I return to You, I become brave. When I stay with You, I begin to learn just how much You love me.

BRAVE THINKING:

Why do some people think God only wants to punish them? Why are they wrong?

⋛ TRUST BALLOON ⋚

*The little troubles we suffer now for a
short time are making us ready for the
great things God is going to give us forever.*
2 CORINTHIANS 4:17

Father, if I fill a balloon, people notice. That balloon gets bigger and brighter. It's hard to hide a filled balloon. It changes people's moods. I want You to fill my *trust balloon* with hope, joy, and peace. Because I trust You, others can see Your gifts in me. Balloons are meant to be used. I'm meant to be useful. Fill me up so I can be useful in helping others see You, meet You, and know You. I don't want to hide; I want to help. I don't want to turn away; I want to trust. I want to jump for joy and pray for peace, and You're the only One who can keep me from hiding and turning away. You do that. Thank You.

BRAVE THINKING:

How does thinking of being filled with
joy and peace like a balloon help?

⋛ ASK ⋚

*You want something but cannot get it, so you fight
for it. You do not get things because you do not
ask for them. Or if you do ask, you do not receive
because your reasons for asking are wrong. You
want these things only to please yourselves.*
JAMES 4:2–3

Dear God, there are things I like and things I want. I can ask an adult for them, trade a friend for them, or save up money to buy them. But when I don't ask You, I have no idea if You want me to have those things. Sometimes You don't want me to have something. I would become selfish if I got what You knew I didn't need. I should ask You and then be satisfied with Your answer. I should ask and then use what You give to help others. I should ask for gifts that please You.

BRAVE THINKING:

Why is it important to ask God
about the things you want?

⋛ TRY TO UNDERSTAND ⋚

*Try to understand other people. Forgive each
other. If you have something against someone,
forgive him. That is the way the Lord forgave you.*

COLOSSIANS 3:13

Father, it would be easy to think that I don't need to try to understand people. After all, You already understand them, so why should I? *Because You told me to.* If I don't at least try to understand people, it's harder to forgive them when they hurt me—and You want me to forgive. Because You understand me, You forgive me. When I was against You, You forgave me. You want me to be courageous enough to treat others the way You have treated me. It would be easy to refuse to forgive other people if You didn't forgive me. It would be easy to hate other people if You hated me. But You love and You forgive. I have no excuse. Help me to love and forgive.

BRAVE THINKING:

How does trying to understand
others make you courageous?

⋛ KEEP ME ⋚

*[Jesus said,] "I am the Vine and you are the branches.
Get your life from Me. Then I will live in you and you
will give much fruit. You can do nothing without Me."*
JOHN 15:5

Dear God, if a flower stem is broken from the
root, the flower will die. If a twig is broken from
a tree, that broken twig becomes a stick. If a
branch is removed from a vine, it is tossed into
a fire because nothing grows from a broken
branch. You are the root, tree, and Vine. You
bring life, and I grow fruit when I stay with You.
The life You bring to me is abundant, it brings
freedom, and it is forever. I can try to do things
on my own, but then I would just be a broken
flower, cracked twig, or a lonely branch. I am
nothing without You, but I can be brave with You.
Keep me close.

BRAVE THINKING:

Why is it important to stay close to God?

⋛ TRUST ⋚

When I am afraid, I will trust in You.
PSALM 56:3

Father, in the middle of night, after a bad dream, and when darkness seems scary, I will trust in You. On the bad days when bullies show up or my test scores are low, I will trust in You. When I don't trust my enemies, my friends, or myself, I will trust in You. When I believe promises can be broken, friendships don't last, and lies are common, I will trust in You. I will trust You with my life, my heart, my soul, my plans, and my needs. I will trust You with all that I am, all that You made me to be, and all that I will be in the future. If I was looking for something to help me and my choice was to fear everything or trust in You, my choice would be easy—I would confidently trust in You.

BRAVE THINKING:

How can trust in God make fear go away?

⋛ WILLING TO SHARE ⋚

There is one who is free in giving, and yet he grows richer. And there is one who keeps what he should give, but he ends up needing more.

PROVERBS 11:24

Dear God, there are people who don't seem to have much money, but they have everything they need. They are generous, compassionate, and kind. They are satisfied with what You give them, and they are willing to share. Others have many things, but they are selfish. They should have everything they need if money could pay for everything they need, but it doesn't. They have many things, but their real needs are never met. They keep what they should give, take what they don't need, and need things they don't want. They can't feel brave when they are never satisfied. Help me accept what You give, because it's just what I need.

BRAVE THINKING:

Why is money a bad way to show how much God loves you?

⮞ SHARING THE GIFT ⮜

God has given each of you a gift.
Use it to help each other.
1 PETER 4:10

Father, I should be satisfied with Your gifts when those gifts let me help others. If You give me exactly what I need, and what I need helps others, then it shouldn't surprise me if You don't want me to have anything that makes me selfish. And I can think of all kinds of things I want that I wouldn't want to share. Help me learn to share with others, because everything You give is meant to be shared. I was made to share things like peace, joy, hope, love, kindness, and faith. If I ever say, "It's mine and you can't have it," then it's probably something I want but not a need. I don't need what You won't give. I don't want what will make me selfish. I want You, the gifts You give, and the wisdom to share.

BRAVE THINKING:

Why should you want what
God wants to give you?

⋛ PAYING ATTENTION ⋚

An understanding mind gets much learning,
and the ear of the wise listens for much learning.
PROVERBS 18:15

Dear God, my mind pays attention to what I read. My ears pay attention to what I hear. You want me to be careful about what I see and listen to. When I pay attention to what I read in Your Word and then learn by listening, I can understand You better. When I pay attention to anyone or anything else, I don't learn as much, I can't understand You more, and I follow You less. *I am easily distracted.* If I can learn from You, I will understand more. When I understand more, I can learn more. By understanding more, I can be more confident when making decisions because I can learn about what You think. I can know You better when I read the Bible.

BRAVE THINKING:

What are some of the benefits
of reading the Bible?

⋛ STRONG ENOUGH TO WAIT ⋚

*Wait for the Lord. Be strong. Let your
heart be strong. Yes, wait for the Lord.*
PSALM 27:14

Father, when I ask You for something, You don't always say yes. Sometimes You say no. You often say to wait. When You say to wait, help me remember that I might not be ready yet. Maybe there are things You need to teach me first. It's possible that someone else might learn something by watching me wait. I can be strong remembering that all kinds of people in the Bible had to wait. You keep the promises You make. You gave rules that I need to keep. You offer gifts that I need to use. And it all starts with being strong enough to wait, strong enough to trust, and strong enough to be patient.

BRAVE THINKING:

How can being impatient make you weak?
How can waiting make you strong?

⋛ LOOK TO YOU ⋚

*"Look to the Lord and ask for
His strength. Look to Him all the time."*
1 Chronicles 16:11

Dear God, You don't want me to be weak; You just want me to know for certain that You make me strong. If I look at what I can do, then I'm not looking at You. If I want to be brave, strong, and courageous, then I need to keep my focus on You. If I want to be strong, then I don't take a day off in my friendship with You. I can look to You in the middle of the night when I can't sleep or when a bad dream wakes me up. I can look to You on the way to school or to a friend's house. I can look to You when I'm alone or with other people. I will always be stronger when I look to You.

BRAVE THINKING:

If you want to be brave, why is it best
to grow in your friendship with God?

⋝ TEMPTATION TELLS LIES ⋜

*You have never been tempted to sin in any
different way than other people. God is faithful.
He will not allow you to be tempted more than
you can take. But when you are tempted, He will
make a way for you to keep from falling into sin.*

1 CORINTHIANS 10:13

Father, a temptation is a suggestion that You don't know what You're talking about. It introduces the idea that You're not perfect. It whispers that my ideas are just as good as Yours. Temptation is always up to no good. It lies to me. It makes me think that maybe You don't care about me. And any person I will ever meet knows temptation. They may also be tricked into thinking You don't care. But when I'm tempted, You have made a way for me to keep from believing lies. You sent Jesus, called Him the Truth, and said I should believe Him.

BRAVE THINKING:

How does God help you avoid temptation?

⋛ WHAT YOU'VE GIVEN ⋚

*I know how to get along with little and how
to live when I have much. I have learned the
secret of being happy at all times. If I am full
of food and have all I need, I am happy. If I
am hungry and need more, I am happy.*

PHILIPPIANS 4:12

Dear God, help me want what You give me. I will be most satisfied when I look forward to the surprise of Your gifts. Even if it seems like what You've given isn't enough or just what I thought I wanted, I can accept that gift with thankfulness. I know that the gift will lead me to trust You more and complain less, and I can be satisfied. None of Your gifts are exactly the same, so I shouldn't be surprised when I don't get the same gift every time. But Your gifts are perfect.

BRAVE THINKING:

Why can you be satisfied when
you let God choose your gifts?

⋜ PEOPLE NEED TO KNOW ⋜

My soul will be proud to tell about the Lord.
Let those who suffer hear it and be filled with joy.
PSALM 34:2

Father, I am here, I am Yours, and I am speaking out. You are amazing, and people need to know that. Use my voice to make You famous to those who've never met You. Use my feet to go places where I can meet those people. Use my heart to want the best for others. When I speak about You, let me be heard, let those who hear discover joy, and let my willingness be pleasing to You. If I'm going to do this, I will need to be brave. You can make me brave. You never ask me to do something alone. You always help, always teach, and always love.

BRAVE THINKING:

Why might it seem embarrassing to talk to people about God? Should it?

⋟ THE BEST JOB ⋞

Whatever work you do, do it with all your heart.
Do it for the Lord and not for men.

COLOSSIANS 3:23

Dear God, when work seems boring or unfair, help me remember who I work for. When I think I'm only cleaning my room because an adult told me I needed to, help me remember that *any* work can be done for You. If I mow the lawn or take out the trash, I can do it to please You. That means I do the best job I possibly can. I have been known just to get by with doing as little as possible. And sometimes I have forgotten to do something I was asked to do. When I do something well, it's nice to hear someone say they thought I did a good job. Someday I hope I can hear that from You.

BRAVE THINKING:

How do you become brave
by working for God?

⇒ SOMETHING TO ME ⇐

Be happy with those who are happy.
Be sad with those who are sad.

ROMANS 12:15

Dear God, sometimes when good things happen to certain people, I get jealous. When certain people are sad, I might be happy because I think they deserve to be sad. When I act like this, I don't look very much like You. People aren't reminded of You when I make everything about me. When good things happen to people, I should be happy for them. When people are sad, I should be sad for them. Here I am again thinking about why I should understand other people. *I need to do that.* I need to care for people enough that when things crash into their world, it means something to me. And when it means something to me, I want to talk to You about it. I should want to help.

BRAVE THINKING:

Why does the way you react to other people matter to God?

⋛ SHOW THEN TELL ⋜

You will show me the way of life.
Being with You is to be full of joy.

PSALM 16:11

Father, when I do things the way *I* want to do things, I'm never very impressed by how things turn out. I don't think You are either. Maybe that's because no matter how much I learn, You're smarter, wiser, and make perfect choices. Since that's true, I don't have to think about whether Your way is best. I don't even have to wonder if I can trust You. *I can.* Show me the way, and give me courage to follow. Keep me close, and fill me with joy. Let me learn what I should do, and give me strength to do it. Help me to become wise and to have the courage to share what You teach. You show; I'll tell.

BRAVE THINKING:

How can the way you think change
when You know that God's way is best?

➤ THE LOAD IS TOO BIG ➤

*[Jesus said,] "Come to Me, all of you who
work and have heavy loads. I will give you rest.
Follow My teachings and learn from Me."*
MATTHEW 11:28–29

Dear God, I carry stuff You never wanted me to
carry. Guilt, worry, and fear cling to me like a
backpack, and they slow me down, wear me out,
and make me sad. This load is too big. Before I
carry this load even one more minute, help me
remember that You don't want me to carry this
load, and You can take what I was never meant to
carry. You can give me rest when I'm so weary I
can't sleep. You can teach me to let go of heavy
burdens. Some people think You make things
harder on people, but that's not anything like
what You say—and You speak truth. Help me to
believe it.

BRAVE THINKING:

Why do you think God has never wanted
you to carry the load of hard things?

⋛ RELATED AND REAL ⋚

We want to see our teaching help you have a true
love that comes from a pure heart. Such love
comes from a heart that says we are not guilty
and from a faith that does not pretend.
1 TIMOTHY 1:5

Father, it's hard to spend much time with pretenders. They don't speak truth. They try to make people think they are something different or better than they are. I get it. Sometimes I want people to think I am more important than I feel. When I trust You, I don't have to pretend. I don't have to be famous—I'm Your child. I don't have to be popular—I'm related to You. I don't have to pretend to be rich—You own everything. And *You love me*. When I really get this, I will feel free to tell people how they can discover the same truth.

BRAVE THINKING:

Why do you think being real and
honest makes you brave?

⋝ A LITTLE BIT BETTER ⋜

*"Be sure you do not do good things in
front of others just to be seen by them."*
MATTHEW 6:1

Dear God, I could wear a T-shirt that says, LOOK AT ME: I DO GOOD STUFF. YOU SHOULD BE IMPRESSED, but that would be embarrassing, and it would look like I was bragging. Probably because I would be bragging! I may not wear the shirt, but I can act in ways that make people think I want them to notice me, that I want to be praised, and that I might be just a little bit better than most. That's not being brave—that's begging for attention. It's me pleading with others to pay attention. That's not what you want me to do. You want me to do good things even when no one's looking. If I want people to think I'm the hero, then I'm not wanting them to notice You.

BRAVE THINKING:

How can doing the right
thing still look like pride?

⋛ MADE TO CARE ⋚

*Think of other people as more
important than yourself.*

PHILIPPIANS 2:3

Father, I love You, and You tell me to love others. If I love You, I pay attention to what You've said and to what You think. If I love others, I pay attention to them too. But if all I can think of is how to make myself important, then I don't have time to love You or others. I'm not even interested. You will always need to be first, but I can't be second. You made me to care about others, and that's why You asked me to think of others' needs as more important than mine. It takes courage to step out of the spotlight and honor You and others. When I put others first, I learn to serve and I'm not as selfish. That sounds like the kind of person You've always wanted me to be.

BRAVE THINKING:

Why does God want You to put the
needs of others before your own needs?

⇒ THE TRUTH ⇐

The Lord hates lying lips, but those
who speak the truth are His joy.

PROVERBS 12:22

Dear God, when I lie, it's not a creative explanation. It's wanting people to believe something I know isn't true. Lies aren't courageous; they are the words of the cowardly. They come from the heart of the embarrassed and guilty. Lies never end in trust. The Bible says You hate lies. If You told lies, it would be hard to trust You. I'm glad You always tell the truth. Maybe the reason You express joy over those who speak truth is because they are acting like You. They sound like You. They even look a little bit more like You. They're doing what You do. It's not always easy to tell the truth when a lie seems a better choice. But it never is. It never has been. It never will be. Give me strength to tell the truth.

BRAVE THINKING:

Why is it the act of the brave to tell the truth?

⪢ LOVE PEOPLE ENOUGH ⪡

So stop lying to each other.
Tell the truth to your neighbor.
EPHESIANS 4:25

Father, when a story starts with "Once upon a time" and ends with "They lived happily ever after," I know that it's made up. This kind of story is fun to listen to, but the people aren't real, what they say didn't happen, and the story was created in the mind of someone with imagination. You want me to stop making things up when I'm supposed to be telling the truth. I don't like it when friends tell me lies. They don't like it when I stop telling the truth. Whether it's to friends, family, or neighbors, help me to speak the truth. You don't want me to do what other people do. Even if everyone else around me lies, You want me to love people enough to tell the truth.

BRAVE THINKING:

How does telling other people the
truth show God's love for them?

⋛ WHAT YOU DO FOR ME ⋚

So we can say for sure, "The Lord is my Helper.
I am not afraid of anything man can do to me."
HEBREWS 13:6

Dear God, people could make fun of me, but You made me Your child. I could be teased, but You love me. Even if I was bullied for following You, I have to remember that You've made a home for me that will be mine forever. You help me, and I need help. Because You help me, I don't have to be afraid. I don't have to be afraid of You. I don't have to be afraid of bullies. I don't have to be afraid of those who might make fun of me. Nothing they can do against me can compare to what You can do for me. No bad thing I ever face will have more meaning than being rescued by You.

BRAVE THINKING:

If God is for You, who could ever
fight against God and win?

⋛ NOT AFRAID ⋚

*You should not act like people who are
owned by someone. They are always afraid.
Instead, the Holy Spirit makes us His sons,
and we can call to Him, "My Father."*

ROMANS 8:15

Father, slaves are people owned by other people.
That wasn't Your plan, but it still happens. Slaves
can't go where they want. They can't chase a
dream. Someone else makes choices for them. If
they don't obey, they are punished. That's what
makes them afraid. That's not You. You make
family members of people who were once someone else's slave. You love them. You give them
big dreams. Your family has hope, and they can
call You Dad. You stay close to Your family and
have only the best plans for them. When I obey
You, it's because I love You and not because I am
afraid of You. I should never be afraid of someone who really loves me. And You love me.

BRAVE THINKING:

How can God's love make you brave?

⋛ ADMIT IT ⋚

If we tell Him our sins, He is faithful and we can depend on Him to forgive us of our sins. He will make our lives clean from all sin.

1 JOHN 1:9

Dear God, I'm asked to follow certain rules every day—rules at school, home, and even in the lunchroom. You have rules too. I don't want to break the rules, but sometimes I do. When I break Your rules, You don't want me to ignore it, pretend it didn't happen, or act like it's no big deal. You gave rules to help protect me, so it's a big deal when I break them. I make You sad, but I also make things harder for myself when I don't admit that You were right and I did the wrong thing. When I do that, You forgive me. Keep me close. Keep me honest.

BRAVE THINKING:

How does it take courage to admit that God is right?

⋛ WISE AND AWAKE ⋚

Keep awake! Watch at all times. The devil is working against you. He is walking around like a hungry lion with his mouth open. He is looking for someone to eat.
1 PETER 5:8

Father, You say Your enemy the devil is also my enemy. If he can't defeat You, then he tries to defeat members of Your family. He tries to hurt You by working against Your children, Christians like me. You don't want me to be defeated, so You remind me to pay attention. You want me to understand those times when the devil is trying to get me to make a bad decision. I can make bad decisions on my own, but Your enemy wants to help me disappoint You whenever he can. You don't want that. Help me to be brave enough to resist Your enemy and wise enough to ask You for help.

BRAVE THINKING:

Why is it wise to pay attention to what God's enemy may be doing when he works against you?

⯈ DIRECTIONS ⯇

*"Watch and pray so that
you will not be tempted."*
MARK 14:38

Dear God, if I don't pay attention, I could get hurt. If I don't look where I'm going, I might trip, bump into stuff, or get distracted. If I don't ask for directions, I will get lost. I've been distracted. I've been lost. I've made bad decisions. The same thing happens when I'm not paying attention to You. I get distracted and don't ask for Your directions. I don't even ask for help. That's when it gets really easy to do what I want to do and ignore You. I don't know exactly where I am or where I'm going. I trip. I fall. I break Your rules. *I don't want to do that.* Help me think of You more, find ways to pay attention, and be brave enough to talk to You when I don't know what to do.

BRAVE THINKING:

Why should God be the One you pay
attention to and talk to when you need help?

⋛ THINK ⋚

*Keep your minds thinking about things in heaven.
Do not think about things on the earth.*

COLOSSIANS 3:2

Father, there are so many things I can think about. A lot of them waste my time, and I don't get any closer to You. Maybe that's why You tell me to stop thinking about those things. You've given me even more to think about in Your Word. I don't think enough about things that are important to You. If this were a classroom, then I'd be guilty of daydreaming. If this were GPS, then I'd not be following directions. If You're asking me to pay attention, then I've said no for too long. Give me the ability to listen and the willingness to obey. I don't want to act as if the things You want me to learn aren't important. You have things I should know, so please help me to think on those things.

BRAVE THINKING:

Why does your mind matter so much to God?

THE RIGHT AMOUNT OF STRENGTH

A man who is right with God
falls seven times, and rises again,
but the sinful fall in time of trouble.
PROVERBS 24:16

Dear God, if I break Your rules, You can forgive me every time I admit I'm wrong and You're right. Every time I stumble, You can help. Every time I get off track, You can show me the right way again. You do this when I'm right with You. This means I want to admit I'm wrong, I want to get back up, and I want to know the best way to go. Some people never admit You're right, and they don't want Your help and don't like Your direction. When they fall, they don't ask for help. They are wrong, and they are stuck. Give me just the right amount of strength to ask You for help. I'm grateful just knowing that I can ask and that You love me enough to help.

BRAVE THINKING:

Why do you need strength to admit you are wrong?

⋛ THINGS TO AVOID ⋚

If you do not have wisdom, ask God for it.
He is always ready to give it to you and
will never say you are wrong for asking.

JAMES 1:5

Father, You have enough wisdom for every person who has ever lived. All I have to do is ask for some and You'll give it to me. Why don't I ask more often? Why do I wait until I'm in trouble before I ask? *Why?* I can learn something from my mistakes, but I can learn more from You. The trouble with learning from mistakes is that mistakes are things I can avoid. If I learn from You, I don't have to make choices that hurt me and disappoint You. The wisdom You have for me is ready to be delivered the moment I ask. You never tell me I should be smarter. You never try to make me think I'm asking a stupid question. Thanks.

BRAVE THINKING:

Why is it better to be wise
than to learn from mistakes?

⇒ BECOMING WISE ⇐

The one who is easy to fool believes everything,
but the wise man looks where he goes.

PROVERBS 14:15

Dear God, some people believe anything. But they can change their opinions when they hear a new idea. I can ask them about something they told me last week, but they've found something new to believe in. That seems foolish. When I follow You, I pay attention to where I'm going, I remember where I've been, and I know how to get in touch with You. You tell me that this shows I am becoming wise. Help me to be brave enough to believe that truth always begins with You. Your truth doesn't change, and You never abandon people who trust Your truth.

BRAVE THINKING:

What can you do today that will help you believe that what God says is what God means?

THOUGHTS GOD NEVER THINKS

Let God change your life. First of all, let Him give you a new mind. Then you will know what God wants you to do. And the things you do will be good and pleasing and perfect.

ROMANS 12:2

Father, I think things that I wish You didn't know about. I have had unkind thoughts about others. I have been jealous. I have wanted things that weren't mine. These are thoughts You never think. *Not even once.* You want to change my life, and that starts with a new way of thinking. As I begin to understand what You want me to do, I won't be thinking unkind thoughts. I won't be jealous or want things that aren't mine. I will learn to do things that build up others and please you. And that's just about perfect.

BRAVE THINKING:

Why is it a good thing to stay away from thoughts God never thinks?

⋛ CHANGE ME ⋚

A man cannot please God unless he has faith.
Anyone who comes to God must believe that He is.
That one must also know that God gives what is
promised to the one who keeps on looking for Him.

HEBREWS 11:6

Dear God, if I find You interesting and that's all, then I haven't come close to pleasing You. If I don't believe in You, then I have made You sad. If I read Bible stories and don't trust the One who made those stories possible, then I haven't allowed Your stories to change me. Coming to You for change means I absolutely believe that You can change me. I have to believe You are real. I have to trust that You keep Your promises. Give me the confidence to believe, trust, and follow. Keep me looking for You. Help me want what You want and do what You've done—things like loving others and forgiving those who've hurt me.

BRAVE THINKING:

Why is it so important to trust God?

⇒ PEOPLE NEED TO HEAR ⇐

Speak with them in such a way they will want to listen to you. Do not let your talk sound foolish. Know how to give the right answer to anyone.

COLOSSIANS 4:6

Father, You don't want me to hide. I can't tell anyone about You if I'm never around other people. When I do talk about You, I should be honest about Your love, forgiveness, and mercy. People need to hear about You, but if they see me being rude or unkind, they will stop listening to me. That kind of talk sounds foolish to them. It makes me sound like I don't really know You and don't know what I'm talking about. I don't want to make things up. Teach me well so I'll know what to say. Help people get ready to hear about You from me.

BRAVE THINKING:

Why is it important for other people
to hear you talk about God?

⮚ BEST KIND OF INVITATION ⮘

*He makes me strong again. He leads me
in the way of living right with Himself
which brings honor to His name.*

PSALM 23:3

Dear God, life is hard. Sometimes it's very hard. I can get confused and want to blame someone for every hard day. I am weak. I know I'm weak. And I don't want to be weak. That's why I need You. With You I learn to make right choices. You can make me strong. And when You do, help me honor You. Help other people honor You when they notice what You've done for me. This adventure that You're taking me on came with the best kind of invitation. You want me to go with You. That's friendship. I've always needed a friend like You. Thanks for loving me enough to call me Your friend.

BRAVE THINKING:

What could you do that would
show You walk with God?

⋛ BRAVE IN THE WAITING ⋛

*You must be willing to
wait without giving up.*
HEBREWS 10:36

Father, some things I don't mind waiting for—like bedtime, showers, and changing socks. But some things are hard to wait for—like chicken nuggets, video games, and time with friends. Sometimes things worth waiting for take a long time—like graduating from high school or learning to drive. Sometimes it's easy to give up, but You say that when I wait for You, I should never give up. You keep promises when others break them. You say, *"Follow Me,"* and then You really lead. I become brave in the waiting. I become courageous thinking about the future You've planned for me. I become strong knowing I can always do what You want me to do. So please help me wait. I don't want to give up. When I'm willing, make me able.

BRAVE THINKING:

Why does waiting seem so hard?
How can waiting make you strong?

⟩ WORTH IT ⟨

*Do not let anyone fool you. Bad people can make
those who want to live good become bad.*

1 CORINTHIANS 15:33

Dear God, You made me to be friendly and have friends. No matter how friendly some people are, they don't want me to have what You're willing to give. They see the good things You do in my life and tell me it's not worth it. They give me new ideas that don't include You. They share new plans, and You're not welcome. They invite me into their world and put up a KEEP OUT sign with Your name on it. Even when I want to do the right thing, they try to talk me out of it. It's hard to follow You and be influenced by people who don't want to follow You. They think I'm wrong for following. Help me to be brave enough to walk with You when others won't.

BRAVE THINKING:

Why is God worth more than
choosing friends who don't like God?

CAN'T HELP TALKING ABOUT IT

I will honor the Lord at all times.
His praise will always be in my mouth.
PSALM 34:1

Father, I was born to honor You in what I say and what I do. Every day when I talk to friends, I am to speak words that honor You. When others don't honor You, that's a perfect time for me to tell them how wonderful You really are. The Bible says that I am to be different. Not *weird* different, but different in a way that makes people wonder why I would honor You over myself. That doesn't seem normal, but it's the right thing to do, and when I see You as wonderful, I can't help talking about it. And when I can't help talking about You, I want You to be honored by my words.

BRAVE THINKING:

Why would some people think it is different to see someone honor God?

⋛ TIME OUT ⋚

We break down every thought and proud thing that puts itself up against the wisdom of God. We take hold of every thought and make it obey Christ.
2 CORINTHIANS 10:5

Dear God, if thoughts are boulders, then You want me to break them down into gravel that can be removed from my mind. A boulder is big and can seem like the most important thing around, but when it's crushed, it's just a pile of rocks. If I break down every thought and everything that looks like it might be more important than You, that's when I can see what's real and what's just rubble. And when my thoughts don't match up with Your wisdom, then bad thoughts must obey You. Whether those thoughts are mine or the thoughts other people share, help me let truth run free and send bad ideas to the rock pile. They need a break.

BRAVE THINKING:

How can your thoughts improve when you match them up to God's wisdom?

⇉ TOTALLY SOLD OUT ⇇

*Your heart should be holy and
set apart for the Lord God.*
1 PETER 3:15

Father, I wear certain clothes only on special occasions. If I have a baseball jersey, I don't wear it when I go swimming. I set some things apart because they serve a purpose only at the right time and in the right place. I'm a bit like that jersey. You set me apart because You created me to do something special. You can't use me if I refuse to be set apart. You can't use me if I think I know more than You. You can't even use me if I think You're wise but I'm too afraid to do what You ask. Being set apart means I am totally sold out to the idea that You have something for me to do, and until I can do it, You'll keep training me.

BRAVE THINKING:

How can you choose to be set
apart so God can use you?

⋛ EVERY SINGLE DAY ⋚

Let us keep looking to Jesus. Our faith comes from Him and He is the One Who makes it perfect. He did not give up when He had to suffer shame and die on a cross. He knew of the joy that would be His later. Now He is sitting at the right side of God.

HEBREWS 12:2

Dear God, faith is Your gift to me. I'm not perfect, but Your faith is. You're the example that never gives up. Help me pay attention to You and Your Son, Jesus. When He died, some people thought He was a criminal, but they were wrong. What seemed embarrassing was the best way to prove that love is real and comes from Your heart to mine. Because I sin, the only approved payment is death, but Jesus paid what I owed. So help me to keep looking to Jesus every single day for the rest of my life.

BRAVE THINKING:

Why is it important to remember
that faith is God's gift to you?

SCARED, WEAK, THEN BRAVE

God is able to do much more than we ask or think through His power working in us.
EPHESIANS 3:20

Father, You want me to be set apart so You can use me. Since You gave me the faith to trust You, I shouldn't find it unusual that You can do things in me and through me that will surprise me. What You do can help others. I could use my imagination to think about all the good things You can do when I am willing to *adventure* with You, but what actually happens is more and better and wiser than my mind can think. It is more than I ask of You. You have the strength to take a scared, weak boy and make him brave. That scared, weak boy is me. I can change, but I need Your help.

BRAVE THINKING:

Why might you try to be brave without God's help? Does it work?

⋛ PROBLEM SOLVED ⋛

*Give all your worries to Him
because He cares for you.*
1 PETER 5:7

Dear God, I can learn so much from You, but when I worry, I have trouble learning because I'm always thinking of something else. My mind won't think of You, at least not for very long. I can be worried about things that insist I think about them. They don't really want You to solve the problem; they just want me to believe the problem can't be solved. If You solve the problem, they know I won't need worry as a sidekick. You know that I never needed worry. I just need to trust. You care for me and You ask me to give You those things that make demands and let You take care of them. Worry never makes me confident. *You do.*

BRAVE THINKING:

How does worry keep you from being brave?

⋟ WHERE I NEED TO START ⋞

*Be right and fair in what you decide. Stand up for
the rights of those who are suffering and in need.*
PROVERBS 31:9

Father, the way I treat people says a lot about
me, but it could say a lot about You if I do it right.
You're fair, and You do what's right. You make
great decisions. That's where I need to start;
and even when I learn some of Your other great
ideas, I need to keep doing the right thing, being
fair with everyone I meet, and making decisions
that please You. Once I learn the basics, help me
pay attention to the struggles other people are
going through. Help me stand up when others
are down. Help me speak up when they can't
speak out. Everyone needs help. May I be courageous enough to stand up, speak up, and help
others just like You do.

BRAVE THINKING:

How can helping others show how
much you have grown with God?

⋛ COOPERATION ⋚

*What does the Lord ask of you but to do
what is fair and to love kindness, and to
walk without pride with your God?*

MICAH 6:8

Dear God, I want to do what You need to have done. I want to help You with plans You have in mind. The truth is, You don't need my help, but You welcome me to Your ideas and give me a purpose. When I cooperate with You, it's easier to be fair with others and to see kindness as an awesome gift that You give and I can share. And when I let You lead, I can't tell You what to do. If I don't know how to do something, it makes sense for me to pay attention to someone who does—*You*. When I don't understand, help me to be willing to ask, "What's next?"

BRAVE THINKING:

Why does it make sense to cooperate with God?

⪦ STOP ME ⪧

If you have been foolish in honoring yourself,
or if you have planned wrong-doing,
put your hand on your mouth.

PROVERBS 30:32

Father, when I want to pull out my trophies to brag, *stop me*. When I think I can do what I want after You've said no, *stop me*. May my hand cover my mouth before I say anything stupid or use my lips to lie. It's nice to hear other people say that I have done a good job, but You don't want me to meet people and tell them why I'm more important. My words can get me into trouble, and I will need You to get me out. If I let You, I can keep from getting myself into so much trouble. I don't need to honor me; I need to honor You. I don't need to do the wrong thing; I need to accept Your help so I can do the right thing.

BRAVE THINKING:

Why do you need God's
help to do the right thing?

⋝ THE CHOICES I MAKE ⋜

*Do your best to add holy living to your faith.
Then add to this a better understanding. As you
have a better understanding, be able to say no
when you need to. Do not give up. And as you wait
and do not give up, live God-like. As you live God-like,
be kind to Christian brothers and love them.*

2 PETER 1:5–7

Dear God, friendship with You started with trust. That changes the way I do things. When I learn more about You, I begin to understand that everything You do has a reason. When I trust Your plan, I can turn down those choices that don't fit. Even when I'm struggling to understand, I don't need to give up. Help me to be patient. Help me to honor You in the choices I make. Help me take everything I discover about You and use it to care for people who love You too.

BRAVE THINKING:

What parts of the verses above do you
think would make you more like Jesus? Why?

⊰ IMPERFECT ⊱

The wisdom that comes from heaven is first of all pure. Then it gives peace. It is gentle and willing to obey. It is full of loving-kindness and of doing good. It has no doubts and does not pretend to be something it is not.
JAMES 3:17

Father, if I said I was perfect, I'd be lying. If I said I wasn't perfect, I would be wise. The Bible says I miss the mark of perfection. *You never have.* With You I don't have to worry or get angry, because You're in control. Your wisdom encourages me to obey, love others, and make right choices. Because You can take away my worries, You can also take my doubts. I am Your child, and You've given me good gifts. Never let me think that pretending I'm something I'm not is a good idea. You love me as I am now and as I become the man You need me to be.

BRAVE THINKING:

Why is it never brave to pretend
to be something you're not?

⋛ STAY ALERT ⋚

Watch and keep awake! Stand true to the Lord.
Keep on acting like men and be strong.

1 CORINTHIANS 16:13

Dear God, if I'm excited about something, I can stay up late, get up early, and pay more attention than I normally would. I can be enthusiastic about sharing what I know. I can get this way when I'm looking forward to something I'm interested in. I can be excited about learning from You, but that will never happen if I'm not looking forward to learning. If I want to grow up to be brave, then I need to keep watching for Your great lessons and stay alert, because I don't want to miss a thing. I will need to stand strong and act like someone who follows You and live like someone who wants to follow You. I will need to know You, and I will want others to know You too.

BRAVE THINKING:

Why is paying attention
a big part of following God?

⋛ FINDING SUCCESS ⋚

Be strong in heart,
all you who hope in the Lord.
PSALM 31:24

Father, when I feel defeated, I don't want to spend time with friends. I don't even want to spend time with You. I feel like I have lost. If there is no chance to find success, then it's hard to want to take big steps in Your direction. That's why You don't want me to feel defeated. You love me, never leave me, and offer to help me. So when You tell me to be strong, You mean it. When You tell me to trust, I'm supposed to trust *You*. There would be no hope if it weren't for You, so help me to hope in You. My strength comes from You, and it's always stronger than my greatest defeat. Help me run to You when I'm discouraged, for You never leave me that way. That's what should always keep me coming back to You.

BRAVE THINKING:

How does it change the way you think of God to know He doesn't want you to stay defeated?

⋛ PEOPLE WILL SEE ⋚

Let no one show little respect for you because you are young. Show other Christians how to live by your life. They should be able to follow you in the way you talk and in what you do.
1 TIMOTHY 4:12

Dear God, I am young. There are more people older than me than there are kids who might look up to me. You say that doesn't matter. I can be an example to anyone. That doesn't mean I can tell people that they have to listen to me; however, I can show them. If I do what You tell me to do, people will see me obeying You. They will see me showing kindness. They will see that loving You is the most important thing to me. It's possible they will show respect for my choices and will honor You. Help me use my words wisely. Help me do the right thing.

BRAVE THINKING:

How can you be a good example to others?

⋛ REMEMBERING LOVE ⋚

Do not be lazy but always work hard. Work for the Lord with a heart full of love for Him.

ROMANS 12:11

Father, I could do things for You, but I don't. You call that laziness. That's the opposite of what You want me to do. When I work, I should work hard. When I work hard, I need to have a reason. That reason is You. I can do my best for You because I love You. My best work will always be because I remember how good You are to me, and each thing I do for You should thank You for Your love for me. When I don't do my best for You, it could be that I've forgotten how much You love me. Please remind me, because I need to be reminded.

BRAVE THINKING:

What does it mean when
you do your best work for God?

⋛ SHARE GOOD THINGS ⋚

I pray that God's great power will make you strong, and that you will have joy as you wait and do not give up. I pray that you will be giving thanks to the Father. He has made it so you could share the good things given to those who belong to Christ.

COLOSSIANS 1:11–12

Dear God, when I pray, I get to ask You for things that will help me stay close to You, but You give me more than I need and ask me to share it with others. If I ask for love, I can share it because Your love never ends. If I ask You to forgive me, I can forgive because You believe in second chances. If I ask You for hope, I can share hope because everyone needs it. Every time I accept one of Your gifts and then share it with others, I get stronger. Help me to be trustworthy when it comes to Your gifts.

BRAVE THINKING:

Why should you remember that
God's gifts are more than you need?

⋛ NOT WHAT HE SAID ⋚

For sure, You will give me goodness and
loving-kindness all the days of my life.
Then I will live with You in Your house forever.

PSALM 23:6

Father, sometimes when I read a verse, I wonder what it would be like if what I read was the opposite of what You said. I might read, "You will take goodness away from me and You will not love me or ever be kind to me. I could never live where You live. It would never be possible." I'm glad that's not what You said, because that would be very depressing. You are the God who brings me goodness. You show me love. And You're kind. You're making a forever home for those who believe in You, and You won't send me away. That sounds so much better. That sounds just like You.

BRAVE THINKING:

Why is it life changing to think
of God as good, loving, and kind?

⇒ EVERYDAY PROTECTION ⇐

Put on the things God gives you to fight with.
EPHESIANS 6:11

Dear God, You don't ask me to attack anyone, but You do ask me to defend. When I am brave, I stand up for You when no one else will. I need to be faithful when people are lacing up their athletic shoes to run away from You. I believe in You when Your enemy tells me I'm being foolish. You gave me armor to protect myself when the enemy shows up. Your armor will always serve me well. You give me truth, righteousness, peace, faith, salvation, and the Bible. Each one protects me, and You want me to use Your protection. It's hard to gain strength when I leave some of Your armor at home. You walk with me. Help me keep the gifts You give me close when we walk together.

BRAVE THINKING:

How can you keep truth, righteousness, peace, faith, salvation, and the Bible close?

⋛ HONORING TOGETHER ⋚

Give great honor to the Lord with me.
Let us praise His name together.

PSALM 34:3

Father, You want me to find other people who will honor You with me. That means my best friends will join me in praising You. You never said I would have to be brave on my own. You can make me brave, and the friends who help me honor You can remind me that bravery is something You want for all of us. I need that kind of encouragement. Together means I am not alone. Together means someone is willing to walk with me. Together means I have You, and it means You have friends for me. The best friends I will ever have will be part of Your family, and they will want to honor You.

BRAVE THINKING:

Why would it be hard to honor God
with friends who don't honor God?

⇒ NEVER LET ME DOWN ⇐

In time of trouble, trusting in a man who is not faithful is like a bad tooth or a foot out of joint.
PROVERBS 25:19

Dear God, when trouble is a same-day delivery, I want to trust You to help me survive each unexpected shipment. Trouble isn't something I order, and it's not something I ask for, but it still shows up. I don't always know how to handle it. You want me to be careful, because when I trust someone who is not You, I may just be asking for more trouble. You can be trusted, but people struggle with trusting You. I can be hurt by people who are not trustworthy. Help me to love people but to trust You. Help me to love You *and* trust You. I have Your promise—You will never let me down.

BRAVE THINKING:

Why is it always a better idea
to trust God over anyone else?

⋛ A WORSHIP GIFT ⋚

Let your bodies be a living and holy gift given to God.
He is pleased with this kind of gift. This is the true
worship that you should give Him.

ROMANS 12:1

Father, You give me all kinds of gifts, and they are all good. They help me get close to You and love other people. I need Your gifts, and You don't hide them from me. But You need a gift from me, and I need to be brave enough to let You have that gift. You want me—my heart, my mind, my soul, and my body. You want to help me know what to think, how to feel, and how to treat my body. You call my gift worship. You say You are pleased when I give this kind of gift. If I can be set apart to be part of Your plan, then my body can be set apart to bring You honor.

BRAVE THINKING:

What can you give God that
He would love to have?

⋛ ONCE TROUBLE SHOWS UP ⋚

He who loves sin loves making trouble.
He who opens his door wide for trouble
is looking for a way to be destroyed.

PROVERBS 17:19

Dear God, trouble can find me anywhere and at any time, but I can avoid many types of trouble. It wouldn't be very wise to invite trouble, because trouble can destroy me. When I break Your rules, it's like asking trouble to drop by for a visit. Once trouble shows up, it doesn't want to leave. Trouble isn't a friend. It doesn't want me to be successful. It wants me to believe You could never love me. Trouble doesn't want me to ask for or accept Your help. The worst part is that when I break Your rules and never admit You're right, then I can become a troublemaker. You don't want that, and neither do I.

BRAVE THINKING:

Who should be friends with trouble? Why?

⋛ REAL BRAVE ⋚

*Trouble and suffering have come
upon me, yet Your Word is my joy.*
PSALM 119:143

Father, trouble and suffering usually travel together, and sometimes they make stops at my house. I don't like it. I might not think I deserve it. When these two show up, help me find my Bible and read. Help me pay attention to Your words, and help me understand how You can use those words to help me most. Trouble isn't a friend, but You can help me learn from it. No one wants to suffer, but You can be a real help when I'm hurting. You never said life would be free of trouble and suffering, but You did say You would help me through every hard day. I can be brave on the hard days, because no matter how hard things get, You are always with me.

BRAVE THINKING:

How can the Bible bring joy
when trouble shows up?

⋛ PAY ATTENTION ⋚

[Jesus said,] "In the world you will have much trouble.
But take hope! I have power over the world!"

JOHN 16:33

Dear God, Jesus said something about trouble, and it was important enough that You made sure it was in the Bible. If it's important to You, then I need to pay attention. What I've learned is that trouble is not a friend, but it will find me—and there are all kinds of trouble. But You don't want me to hide, be afraid, or run away. There is no trouble that You can't take care of. There is no suffering that can make You stop loving me. You have power over everything, so I don't need to worry. I don't need to be afraid. I don't need to be without hope. I just don't. You love me, and that changes how I act when trouble comes.

BRAVE THINKING:

Why is it important to remember
that you don't have to be afraid
when you find trouble or it finds you?

⋛ WAIT FOR AN ANSWER ⋚

My Christian brothers, you should be happy
when you have all kinds of tests. You know
these prove your faith. It helps you not to
give up. Learn well how to wait so you will be
strong and complete and in need of nothing.

JAMES 1:2–4

Father, brave boys live through trouble because they have Your help. You want me to choose joy over despair, peace over worry, and love over fear. For You can use trouble to make my faith strong. Times of trouble make me patient and give me time to worship You while I wait for Your answer. I will become strong as I trust in You and wait for You. You bring good to those who love You and follow You through trouble to triumph. This is called endurance, and it's part of Your plan for me.

BRAVE THINKING:

How can hard days help
you trust God more?

⇒ WHEN I BECOME WEAK ⇐

*I pray that God's great power will
make you strong, and that you will
have joy as you wait and do not give up.*

COLOSSIANS 1:11

Dear God, You don't ask me to head to the gym and spend hours proving I have everything I need to do things all by myself. If I don't need You, then I'm not really strong; I just think I am. And when I think I am strong and don't need You, that's exactly when I become weak. But when I wait for You to bring help, I learn more than I ever thought I could. I'm used to seeing people try to prove they are better by how successful they are at almost anything. I am strongest when I follow where You lead, wait for Your answers, and know for certain that You can take care of everything.

BRAVE THINKING:

Why is following God more important
than being the best at something else?

⋛ HIS EXAMPLE ⋚

*Now the God Who helps you not to give up and
gives you strength will help you think so you
can please each other as Christ Jesus did.*

ROMANS 15:5

Father, I don't have to give up, for You help me
endure. You give me Your strength when I'm
weak. You give me Your thoughts when I only
want to think about myself. You gave me family
and friends to care for. So when I trust You
and love them, I'm doing what Jesus did when
He came to live here. His example is important.
He was strong enough to really care for other
people. He fed them and healed them and loved
them. Other people had the same example,
and they love me and care for me. I'm glad they
learned enough from You to help me so I can
help others.

BRAVE THINKING:

How does God use endurance to
help you learn how to help others?

⋟ I AM NOT AFRAID ⋞

*There is no fear in love. Perfect love puts
fear out of our hearts. People have fear
when they are afraid of being punished.*

1 JOHN 4:18

Dear God, Your love accepts me before it teaches me. It embraces me before it asks me to embrace others. Love is kind, and when You love me this way, I am not afraid. You don't want me to be afraid. You don't even want people to try to convince me that I should be afraid. Your love sends fear away. Your love doesn't punish—it corrects. That means You aren't angry with me, but You want to point me in the right direction so I don't make the same mistakes over and over again. Your love wants the best for me and is willing to point out those things that will never be the best. Help me pay attention to Your love.

BRAVE THINKING:

What is the difference between
punishment and correction?

THE IMPORTANCE OF FOLLOWING

The one who keeps looking into God's perfect Law and does not forget it will do what it says and be happy as he does it. God's Word makes men free.

JAMES 1:25

Father, You created a law that You want Your family to follow. Cities and schools have rules too. It doesn't always seem fair to follow all the rules and laws I'm told to follow. When it comes to Your law, the reason to follow is important. When I do what You ask me to do, I'm free to do exactly what You made me to do. Your greatest law is for people who love You to love others. When I love others, they don't need to be afraid of me. They don't need to wonder if I will take something that belongs to them. Loving others and wanting Your best for them is a courageous thing to do. You do that for me.

BRAVE THINKING:

How does love help you obey God's law?

⋛ LOOK UP ⋚

*The heavens are telling of the greatness
of God and the great open spaces
above show the work of His hands.*

PSALM 19:1

Dear God, I can look at the sky and see the sunrise, clouds, or even stars. No one can make those things but You. The moon is a reminder that You are great. You've made things I will never see. You've created things that surprise and amaze me. When I look beyond the streetlights, porch lights, and flashlights, I see things You created that make me believe that no one will ever be greater than You. When people need a reminder that You exist and take care of us, they just need to look out and look up. There are reminders everywhere. The brave will see the proof and believe. The fearful might still think they are alone. That makes me sad. Thanks for Your beautiful reminders.

BRAVE THINKING:

What part of nature reminds
you of God's goodness?

⋗ THEY NEED TO KNOW ⋞

The person who is not a Christian does not understand these words from the Holy Spirit. He thinks they are foolish. He cannot understand them because he does not have the Holy Spirit to help him understand.
1 CORINTHIANS 2:14

Father, the foolish are fearful. They don't know what to believe, so the only thing they believe is the lies that fear repeats. I never want their fear to stop me from being confident enough to tell them about You. They need to know that You can teach them how to really live. They need to know You love them. They need to understand You. I can learn every day when Your Spirit teaches what seems hard to understand. When I became a Christian, You invited me to give up my fear and become willing to follow You. That's when You began to teach me. That's when I began to understand.

BRAVE THINKING:

Why is it so important to let God teach you?

⋛ WHEN PEOPLE PRAY ⋚

Pray for me also. Pray that I might open my
mouth without fear. Pray that I will use the
right words to preach that which is hard
to understand in the Good News.

EPHESIANS 6:19

Dear God, I can pray for others, and they can pray for me. I want them to. I need them to. It doesn't always seem easy to tell other people about You, but when people are praying for me, I can speak about You without being afraid. When people pray for me, You can answer their prayers by giving me the right words to say. These prayers can help people understand You better when I'm brave enough to speak Your truth and they are willing to listen. I can share the Good News, and prayer will always help me say what needs to be said.

BRAVE THINKING:

Have you ever asked anyone to pray for you when you plan to tell someone about Jesus? Why?

⋛ DIFFERENT IDEAS ⋚

Be careful that no one changes your mind and faith by much learning and big sounding ideas. Those things are what men dream up. They are always trying to make new religions. These leave out Christ.

COLOSSIANS 2:8

Father, someone could tell me that You don't really love me all the time, and I might believe it. *But it wouldn't be true.* Someone could say that You don't really help people who ask for help, and I might wonder if it's true. *But it's not.* Lots of people have ideas they want to believe, but if those ideas are different from Your truth, then they are a lie. They aren't worth believing. One of the easiest ways I can understand if something is true or not is whether the idea leaves You out. I never want to leave You out, behind, or to the side. Walk with me and teach me Your truth.

BRAVE THINKING:

Why does real truth never leave out God?

⋟ AMAZING PLANS ⋞

Open my eyes so that I may see
great things from Your Law.
PSALM 119:18

Dear God, when I read the Bible and I see what You want me to do, I might think that Your rules are for other people but maybe not me. You want me to ask for eyes that see, a mind that understands, and a willingness to obey Your laws. You say that when I pay attention, I will see great things. That means Your laws aren't supposed to depress me but are to make me grateful that You have always wanted the best for me. I will need help to see how amazing Your plan actually is. Help me remember that Your plan for me is so much better than my guesses. Help me to see You for the good God You've always been and to honor You.

BRAVE THINKING:

Why do you need God's help to see
how wonderful His commands are?

⋛ CAN'T PICK A FAVORITE ⋚

*For the Lord is good. His loving-kindness
lasts forever. And He is faithful to all
people and to all their children-to-come.*

PSALM 100:5

Father, if I picked ten people and asked You to choose a favorite, I would never be able to give someone a trophy because You don't have favorites. The love You have for people does not depend on anything other than Your willingness to love. I can't pay anything to make You love me more. Doing extra good things won't make You love me more. Being born into a specific family won't make You love me more. You just love me. And You don't stop loving me. You are kind. And You've always been kind. You are faithful. And You will always be faithful. Ten people in one room can all discover that You can't love them more than You do and You won't love them less.

BRAVE THINKING:

Since God loves everyone, how should
that change the way you treat people?

⇉ JESUS FACED MORE ⇇

Sinful men spoke words of hate against Christ.
He was willing to take such shame from sinners.
Think of this so you will not get tired and give up.

HEBREWS 12:3

Dear God, You are kind to people even when they are not kind to You. Your Son loved people when they could speak only words of hate to Him. Jesus endured more than most people ever will, and even though He could have said He had enough, He was willing to die for my sin. I don't know anyone else who would do that for me. What Jesus did for me was strong enough to save me, and that can make me brave. No matter how hard things get for me, Jesus faced more. You have never wanted me to get weary and give up, because Jesus never did either.

BRAVE THINKING:

Why is it easy to think about giving up?
Why is Jesus' example important?

⋛ JUST THE BEGINNING ⋚

Everything that was written in the Holy Writings
long ago was written to teach us. By not giving up,
God's Word gives us strength and hope.

ROMANS 15:4

Father, it's easy to give up on things that seem too hard. But sometimes the only way to know something really well is to keep learning even when it's hard to understand at the beginning. If I want to be an astronaut, I need to know math. That means I can't stop learning math once I know what two plus two equals. That's just the beginning. It's a wonderful thing to know that You love me, and that's a great start, but You have a lot to teach me, and what I can learn can make me strong. Love is just the first step. You wrote words to teach. I read Your words to learn. I am braver when I learn what You teach.

BRAVE THINKING:

How does it help to know that
everything God put in the Bible is
something you can learn from?

⚡ I BELIEVE ⚡

I have put my trust in God.
I will not be afraid.
PSALM 56:4

Dear God, when I decided to trust You, You gave me one of Your gifts—bravery. I believe in You, and I have no reason to fear. I have faith, and worry is uncomfortable. When I'm afraid, I believe everything is out of control, I think that bad things will happen and there will be no one to help me, and I don't believe I can trust anyone. Faith tells me that You are my Helper when bad things happen, You are in control, and I can trust You to take care of me. When other people let me down, remind me that You never have. When You make a promise, I will need to remember that You always keep Your promises. When I want the best, I can be satisfied that I put my trust in You.

BRAVE THINKING:

What can you do to make
worry uncomfortable?

⇒ I'VE SEEN IT FOR MYSELF ⇐

O taste and see that the Lord is good.
How happy is the man who trusts in Him!

PSALM 34:8

Father, You don't need me to agree that You're good. You're good whether I think You are or not. But when I give You my trust, that's when I can see how good You really are. When I trust You, I am satisfied that I made a good decision. And every day I can make that same choice. Every day You fill me with good things. It's up to me to recognize all the good things You have for me. It's like tasting the best food; but with You, I don't need to be worried about getting too full of the good things You give. I can share the extra. People need to know that You're good. You want me to be someone who can tell them because I've seen Your goodness for myself.

BRAVE THINKING:

What can you do today that will help
you recognize the goodness of God?

⋛ EXTRA HELP ⋚

The angel of the Lord stays close to those who fear Him, and He takes them out of trouble.

PSALM 34:7

Dear God, You keep me company. You never leave me, and You don't turn Your back on me. Sometimes You bring company. You created angels, and when I am facing trouble, You send them to help me. I never see them, but they are another one of Your wonderful gifts. When I trust You, that's when You send help that I never deserve but really need. You are close to me. Help me stay close to You. You rescue, and I need to be rescued. I don't go anywhere without You, and I like Your company. May I use my mouth to ask for help and my mind to remember that You do help, and know that my heart is where my Helper lives.

BRAVE THINKING:

Why should you want God to stay close to you?

⟩ PULL SIN WEEDS ⟨

*Let us put every thing out of our lives that keeps us
from doing what we should. Let us keep running
in the race that God has planned for us.*
HEBREWS 12:1

Father, when I want to hold on to the things You tell me to let go of, I'm asking for trouble. I need to run toward You and away from the choice to sin. You want to help me pull *sin weeds* so that You can grow new life in me. You aren't asking me to give up something I need—You already give me everything I actually need. This life is a race, and I need to run with Your love and favor. Help me turn my back on trouble so I can see the incredible things You want me to have.

BRAVE THINKING:

What *sin weeds* are hardest to pull? Why?

⋛ EVEN THOUGH I SUFFER ⋚

We think of those who stayed true to Him as happy even though they suffered. You have heard how long Job waited. You have seen what the Lord did for him in the end. The Lord is full of loving-kindness and pity.

JAMES 5:11

Dear God, people who have a lot of joy have usually suffered more than most. It's not like they love suffering or are looking for trouble. They are just brave enough to know that You will still be there at the end of every bad day. Job struggled, and in the end You chose to bless Him. David struggled, and You made him a king. Joseph struggled, and You helped him save people who were starving. You give what I can't afford, care more than anyone ever has, and love me when I struggle to love. When I suffer, give me Your joy.

BRAVE THINKING:

Why does your future never
depend on your past?

⤜ THE GREAT TAKEAWAY ⤛

*Dear friends, your faith is going to be
tested as if it were going through
fire. Do not be surprised at this.*
1 PETER 4:12

Father, gold becomes shiny and smooth when it
goes through fire. The part that will not make it
shiny rises to the top, and it can be taken away
from the gold to make it pure. You said that my
faith in You would be tested the same way. Hard
times help me learn from You. I become brave
when I see how You take me through suffering. I
shouldn't be surprised that this is what happens.
It shouldn't be the news of the day to learn that
there are things in my life that You want to take
away. They are things I have never needed. They
are things You've never wanted for me. Help me
to let go of what could never make me pure.

BRAVE THINKING:

Why do you need God's help
to get through suffering?

⇒ NO NEED TO GUESS ⇐

May the Lord lead your hearts into the love of God.
May He help you as you wait for Christ.
2 Thessalonians 3:5

Dear God, when I don't know where to go, You lead me to Your love. When I search on my own, I never really understand where You're leading me and why I need to go there. I can think that You want me to figure out what to do on my own, *but You don't.* You don't hide Your love, and You don't want me to guess what I need to do next. You know I need wisdom, and You promise to make wisdom a very important gift. Teach me. Lead me. Help me. Give me what I need most—and *what I need most is You.* Help me to be brave enough to take steps in Your direction and walk with You, because I am certain You know the way.

BRAVE THINKING:

What should you do if you want God to lead?

⋛ LOVE RECOGNIZED ⋚

Do not always be thinking about your own plans only.
Be happy to know what other people are doing.

PHILIPPIANS 2:4

Father, what are You doing? You have plans, and I'd like to know what they are. You made people, and each person has a story. It's not unusual for me to think that what I'm doing is the most important thing. Sometimes I don't pay attention to the stories happening all around me. My family and friends need to know that I care about both the good things and bad things that are happening in their lives. Your main rule is to love people. They can't recognize Your love if they don't see it in me. When someone needs to share something with me, keep my ears open, my heart connected, and the love You've given me available to each storyteller. Let me listen to You—and then others.

BRAVE THINKING:

Why did God create listening to be a
part of how you show love to others?

⋗ ENJOY EVERY MOMENT ⋖

*Do not let yourselves get tired of doing good.
If we do not give up, we will get what is
coming to us at the right time.*

GALATIANS 6:9

Dear God, I don't want to take a day off from doing the right thing. I don't want to take a vacation in the land of *Give Up.* I want to believe there's a day coming when You'll show me something better. You have even more gifts for me, but I'll have to wait. Don't let me rush Your *right time*, for You have enough good gifts for me to enjoy right now. Help me enjoy every moment. And while I wait, help me to find joy in doing what You want me to do. Help me never to give up when I need to show up. Help me never to sit down if You need me to stand up—with You, for You, and beside You.

BRAVE THINKING:

After reading the verse and prayer,
how can You describe being bold?

⇒ THE RIGHT THINGS ⇐

*Everyone of us will give an answer
to God about himself.*
ROMANS 14:12

Father, what did I do today? That's more of a question for me—You already know. Sometimes You want me to think about how I spend my time. In fact, someday You'll ask me about it. Because I want to be brave, I also want to do the right thing so that when You ask me how I used the time You gave me, I will be able to tell You things that will please You. I don't want to tell You about things I wish I'd never done. I want to accept Your help so I can be strong enough to do the kinds of things You want me to do. These are the things You will want to hear about someday.

BRAVE THINKING:

What can you do today that will help
you make the right choices tomorrow?

⋛ THE WANDERER ⋛

*The Lord is my Shepherd. I will
have everything I need.*
PSALM 23:1

Dear God, a shepherd doesn't make sheep defend themselves, find their own food, or take care of themselves. Since You're my Shepherd, I have everything I need. *Everything.* You defend me. You feed me. You take care of me. A good shepherd never leaves sheep alone, and *You are my Good Shepherd.* Sheep aren't brave on their own. They wander away, they get lost, and they need to be rescued. *That's me.* Your sheep become brave when they rely on the Good Shepherd. *That's You.* Help me never to be ashamed to be one of Your sheep. Being a sheep means I stay close to the Shepherd. *I get to stay close to You.*

BRAVE THINKING:

Why can you celebrate being
compared to a sheep?

⋛ HELP ME SAY THAT ⋚

When pride comes, then comes shame,
but wisdom is with those who have no pride.
PROVERBS 11:2

Father, I might think I'm pretty good at some things. I might even think I'm the best. When I make a big deal out of how good I am at something, I might come face-to-face with someone who is better. People might make fun of me. I might be angry, embarrassed, and ashamed. When I let You be famous, I'm making a wise choice. You really are the best at everything, and You want to teach me. I can't learn if I think I know it all, can do it all, and want to brag to all. I stumble and fall, and when I do, help me remember that You don't push me away, make fun of me, or embarrass me. You are amazing. Help me say that more often.

BRAVE THINKING:

Why is bragging a foolish thing
to do for a Christian?

⋛ WHEN I. . . ⋚

The path of the lazy man is grown over with thorns,
but the path of the faithful is a good road.
PROVERBS 15:19

Dear God, when I don't make the choice to fol-low You, I'm making a choice not to follow You. When I don't make the choice to learn from You, I'm not learning from You. When I don't live for You, no one sees You in what I say and do. When I don't walk with You, my path forward is dan-gerous and I don't understand where to go. But when I make the choice to follow You, I am led in a good direction. When I make the choice to learn from You, I am taught. When I live for You, people notice. When I walk with You, I know there really is a destination. When I am faced with a choice, help me bravely to trust You to help me make it. Then? Help me do it!

BRAVE THINKING:

Why is the Christian life filled
with so many choices?

⋛ LEARNING WISDOM ⋚

Fools hate wisdom and teaching.
PROVERBS 1:7

Father, sometimes wisdom seems like someone trying to tell me what to do or like someone saying that what I'm doing is wrong. Teaching can seem like something that takes me away from fun things. People who don't have wisdom are said to be foolish, but most people don't seem to want wisdom, and that is foolish. Help me never to make the mistake of thinking that being smart is the same as being wise. I can know lots of things but never be wise enough to do the right things with what I know. Knowledge knows the parts of a car, but wisdom knows how to fix the car. Knowledge knows the ingredients in a meal, but wisdom knows how to cook the meal. Knowledge knows some things about You, but wisdom knows You can be trusted and then trusts You. Help me learn. Help me to be wise.

BRAVE THINKING:

What are some differences
between knowledge and wisdom?

⋛ STUBBORN ⋚

*[Jesus said,] "You do not want to
come to Me so you might have life."*
JOHN 5:40

Dear God, I can be so stubborn. Sometimes when someone asks me to do something, I'm determined to show that I don't have to do it. I don't want to do it. And if I do what they ask, I make sure they know I didn't want to do it. This kind of stubbornness must make You very sad. You don't ask me to do things that You won't help me to do or that are bad for me. You always know what I need and have a plan. Following You helps me live a good life. But Jesus knew there were many people who were stubborn too. They didn't want to let Him lead. They didn't believe He offered a better life. They were wrong. So am I whenever I refuse to follow when You offer to lead.

BRAVE THINKING:

How is being stubborn unhelpful to Christians?

⋛ ENOUGH TO KNOW BETTER ⋜

*Those who do what their sinful old
selves want to do cannot please God.*
ROMANS 8:8

Father, when I decide that anything I want to do is a better choice than obeying You, I can't expect You to be happy about it. When I worry, I am saying that You can't be trusted, *but You can*. When I choose to do what I want to do, I am saying that I'm more important than You, *but I'm not*. When I choose to listen to other people more than You, I'm saying their opinions are worth more than Yours, *but they never will be*. And all of this is worse when I have learned enough about You to know better. It's worse because I know what I'm doing when I turn away from You. That's something You never do to me.

BRAVE THINKING:

Why is it impossible to be
brave while disobeying God?

⁋ THE GOOD CONVERSATION ⁋

*The prayer from the heart of a
man right with God has much power.*

JAMES 5:16

Dear God, prayers can be easy to say, but if I never admit You're right when I pray, then I can't really expect You to say yes to my prayers. And if I really think I know everything, then what's the reason to pray? But when I get to know You, learn to serve You, and choose to obey You, my prayer becomes the conversation You want it to be. You hear my prayer, and I learn the things You want me to know. When I get to know You, I learn to pray prayers that You want to answer. For instance, I might choose to pray for something someone needs rather than something I want. I don't want to pray the prayer of a stranger. I want to pray the prayer of Your friend.

BRAVE THINKING:

How can prayers show that you're
growing up as a Christian?

⇒ JOY FILLED ⇐

*Be full of joy always because you belong
to the Lord. Again I say, be full of joy!*
PHILIPPIANS 4:4

Father, because I'm Yours, I can choose to take the joy You give or I can choose to live in sadness. Even though it doesn't make sense, I sometimes choose sadness. Joy believes You can be trusted. Sadness believes no one can be trusted. When I accepted Your Son, I became Your child. I am for You. You are with me. We are family. That means I can celebrate. I can allow You to fill my heart with joy because You want me to be filled with joy. Give me the courage to choose joy every time.

BRAVE THINKING:

Why does God want you to be filled with joy?

⇒ GENTLE, NOT WEAK ⇐

Let all people see how gentle you are.
PHILIPPIANS 4:5

Dear God, picking on people is not what You do. When You sent Your Son, Jesus, He was gentle, humble, and innocent. Some people think looking, acting, and sounding tough makes them important. They think people respect them more when they push others around. They might make people afraid, but people don't respect them. I wouldn't have the same friendship with You if You acted like a bully. I don't want to be afraid of You; I just want to honor You. May people see me as gentle and compassionate. This is not weakness; this is strength. This is not the sign of a wimp— it's the heart of bravery. Gentleness shows love, which is at the top of Your list of rules. Help me make gentleness visible.

BRAVE THINKING:

Why does God see gentleness as
more valuable than being a bully?

TRADING WORRY FOR ANSWERS

Do not worry. Learn to pray about everything. Give thanks to God as you ask Him for what you need.

PHILIPPIANS 4:6

Father, worry is me talking to myself about things I *can't* control. Prayer is me talking to You about things You *can* control. No wonder You don't want me wasting time by worrying. And when I really understand how much You can help, not only can I move worry out of my thoughts, but I can be grateful to You for the help. This is a good reminder to use my time talking to You about things that concern me. Help me exchange worry for answers, despair for prayer, and concerns for conversation with You.

BRAVE THINKING:

Why should you remember that God controls everything?

⋛ UNDERSTANDING PEACE ⋚

*The peace of God is much greater than the human
mind can understand. This peace will keep your
hearts and minds through Christ Jesus.*

PHILIPPIANS 4:7

Dear God, peace is a brave response. I can be calm when I trust You to take care of things even when things seem out of control. Peace isn't just the ability to sleep well because I don't have anything that could worry me. Peace happens when I believe that You are faithful on all sides of trouble—before, during, and after. Having peace is brave because I know there are more answers to discover once the storm is over. Having peace means walking with You through the storm, knowing there is no storm that's bigger than You. Best of all, peace is another gift You offer to Your family. Help me choose it even when I don't understand the trouble I walk through. I want to stay close because I need to experience Your peace.

BRAVE THINKING:

How is peace different than not
experiencing trouble?

⋛ THINK ⋚

Christian brothers, keep your minds thinking about whatever is true, whatever is respected, whatever is right, whatever is pure, whatever can be loved, and whatever is well thought of. If there is anything good and worth giving thanks for, think about these things.

PHILIPPIANS 4:8

Father, some thoughts are true and some aren't. Not everything I could think about is worth the time and effort. Some thoughts can get me into trouble and some are unkind. I should think about things that are true—*they match what Your Word says*. I should think about things that are respected—*they have Your traits*. I should think about things that are right and pure—*they champion Your plans and care for Your people*. I should think about how I can love others—*it's what You do*. I can think about other things that are good and worthy. That should keep me busy. Help me learn what to think about.

BRAVE THINKING:

Why should you know what
God wants you to think about?

⇒ SOMEONE WHO FOLLOWS ⇐

*Keep on doing all the things
you learned and received and heard
from me. Do the things you saw me do.*

PHILIPPIANS 4:9

Dear God, when I know the right thing and do the right thing, help me to keep doing the right thing. You don't ask me to be kind once just so I know what that feels like. You want me to be kind and then keep being kind. You want me to love others and then keep loving them. You want me to trust You and keep trusting You. This is called obedience. It's what I need to do—for You, for me, for others. People can read how to follow You, but they also need to see someone who actually follows You. Let me be someone others see following You.

BRAVE THINKING:

What are some of the reasons to keep
doing the things you learn in the Bible?

⋛ TAKEN CARE OF ⋚

There is a special time for everything. There is a time for everything that happens under heaven.
ECCLESIASTES 3:1

Father, things will not always stay the same, and that can seem scary. When things are good, I can be happy. When things are bad, I can be sad, but maybe I'm not thinking about things as You do. You say there are times for everything and that even the difficult times can help me grow. If I don't trust You in each challenge I face, then I might not learn what You want to teach. If I am brave, I will trust You to help me through each new struggle. This helps me understand that You are a very big God who can handle very big problems when I am overwhelmed. You said there is a time for everything that happens under heaven. Help me remember that there's nothing that surprises You, and there's nothing You can't take care of.

BRAVE THINKING:

Why does God allow life to be challenging?

⇒ NO SECRET ⇐

We speak without fear because
our trust is in Christ.
2 CORINTHIANS 3:12

Dear God, why would You want me to keep my friendship with You a secret? *You wouldn't.* You want me to be brave enough to tell people that I'm Your student. I cannot love anyone the way You want me to love them if I don't talk about You. I have good news, and You want me to share it. You can help people, teach people, and love people, but they need to be introduced to You. That's what Christians do—introduce people to You. They aren't afraid to do that either. I will tell Your story from Your Word. I will explain what You've done in my life. You have changed me, and the last thing I want to do is be afraid to tell people about the Change Maker. Make me bold, make me strong, and fill me with Your words.

BRAVE THINKING:

Why are you considered strong
when you talk about God?

⋗ THE FUEL TO KEEP GOING ⋖

*"But you be strong.
Do not lose strength of heart."*
2 CHRONICLES 15:7

Father, You told me to be strong and said You would give me Your strength. Then You told me not to lose that strength. The key is to stay close to You. When someone in the Bible was brave and strong, it's because You made them strong. When they were weakest, that's when they needed to spend time with You. You give any strength I have the fuel to keep going. You make me brave, and I am bravest when I follow Your plan, accept Your direction, and talk to You often. I am weak. You are strong. You want me to use Your strength to be confident enough to follow You every day of my life.

BRAVE THINKING:

Why does God take weak people
and make them strong?

⇒ I BELIEVE ⇐

Now faith is being sure we will get what we hope for. It is being sure of what we cannot see.

HEBREWS 11:1

Dear God, even when I can see clearly, there are some things I can't see. I can't actually see love, but I can recognize love when someone is in demonstration mode. I can't see wind, but I see what wind does. I can't see faith, but I know faith believes in something it has never seen. Faith is sure You exist even when it has never seen You. Faith believes there is a place where You live and where Christians will one day live with You. Faith has no doubt it's worth following You because You have always been trustworthy. Help me to see what's real, accept what's true, and live like those things matter—*because they do*. Let me declare: You are a good God, and *I believe*.

BRAVE THINKING:

Why should you believe God in everything?

BETTER THAN A BUCKET LIST

" 'For I know the plans I have for you,'
says the Lord, 'plans for well-being and not
for trouble, to give you a future and a hope.' "
JEREMIAH 29:11

Father, I can set goals for things I want to do in the future. Some people call long-term goals a bucket list because they know they have a limited time to get them done. You don't have a bucket list. Your plans for me get done as long as I don't stand in Your way. You could make me do anything You want, but that's not Your way. You point me in the right direction, but I will need to walk in Your direction—and it's good. Your plan takes care of me, gives me a good future, and says that hope trusts in Your promises. You have always had a better adventure for me. Your plans are better than a bucket list.

BRAVE THINKING:

Why are God's future plans for
you better than your plans?

⋛ MORE PROOF ⋚

They who wait upon the Lord will get new strength.
They will rise up with wings like eagles. They will run
and not get tired. They will walk and not become weak.

ISAIAH 40:31

Dear God, if I needed more proof that You make me strong, You've given me a verse in the book of Isaiah that makes it clear. When I am patient and follow You, I find strength like an eagle flying over a river or a runner crossing the finish line. Following You isn't a burden, and I'll never be disappointed when I do. This promise isn't just for me; it's for everybody. I can tell people because they will need to know. Help me wait for You. Help me become strong. I'm willing to go on Your adventure. I am ready to follow. Help me walk forward when You say it's time to go.

BRAVE THINKING:

Why should you never be disappointed
when you choose to follow God?

⋟ I AM SAFE ⋞

"Be strong and have strength of heart. Do not be afraid or shake with fear because of them. For the Lord your God is the One Who goes with you. He will be faithful to you. He will not leave you alone."

DEUTERONOMY 31:6

Father, may I be strong and brave. May I not be afraid, for You go with me. You've always been faithful. You don't leave. You don't abandon. These are simple phrases, but they are sometimes hard to believe. At times I *feel* like I'm alone and wonder if You've abandoned me. Sometimes I don't trust You. And sometimes I don't *feel* brave. That's the truth, but it's not Your truth. These are things I *feel*, but they don't match the truths I read in the Bible. Your Word says I can *know* I don't have a reason to worry or be afraid when I trust You. You are with me. You said so.

BRAVE THINKING:

What makes it hard for you to be brave?

⇉ HELP ME FORGIVE ⇇

A man of anger starts fights, and a man with a bad temper is full of wrong-doing.
PROVERBS 29:22

Dear God, when I'm angry, it's not hard for other people to become angry too. When people make me mad, I often make the wrong choice. Anger is an emotion You gave me. Anger stands up for injustice, but when anger is the first choice I make, then I can't forgive or love others; instead, I feel like a victim. When I'm brave enough to forgive someone, I'm not a victim; I'm an overcomer. I can't accept Your gifts of peace, love, and compassion if I'm convinced that everyone else is mean. When I can't forgive others, I never feel forgiven by You. I need to admit that You're right and I'm wrong when I don't want to forgive. I don't want to start fights. I don't want a bad temper. I want to be forgiven. Please help me.

BRAVE THINKING:

Why does a bad temper never
look like God's example?

⇉ LOVE ⇇

*[Jesus said,] "If you love each other,
all men will know you are My followers."*
JOHN 13:35

Father, love never stays angry, always forgives, and refuses to pay back a bad choice with another bad choice. The Bible even says that people should recognize those who follow You by their choice to love instead of hate. When Your followers don't love other people, it's hard to convince others that they follow You. If people believe that You love and forgive, they expect me to love and forgive. When I don't love and forgive, people might think I don't actually follow You or that my bad choice doesn't make You sad. Two things I know for sure: You want me to love others, and You want me to trust You enough to obey. It's very hard to follow You if I don't love other people. That's what You said, and it's what I need to believe.

BRAVE THINKING:

Why is love such an important
part of the Christian life?

﹥ LOVE UNDERSTOOD ﹤

Hope never makes us ashamed because the love of God has come into our hearts through the Holy Spirit Who was given to us.

ROMANS 5:5

Dear God, You want me to become different when You introduce me to Your love. You said that You loved me enough that You sent Jesus to pay the price for my sin. Jesus showed love to people throughout His life. You sent Your Spirit to make sure I understood Your love. I have no excuse not to know that You love me and no reason to feel unloved by You. My trust in You does not make me ashamed, because You said that love sends fear away. I must be brave enough to really believe that You love me. You don't need time to get to know me. You already know everything about me. Help me to love You and share Your love.

BRAVE THINKING:

Why would someone think that God doesn't love them?

⋛ NO LONGER A RUNAWAY ⋚

*A man will not stand by doing what
is wrong, but the root of those who
are right with God will not be moved.*

PROVERBS 12:3

Father, if I make a wrong choice, I'll always run from my choice. If I lie, I can be afraid that someone will find out and I'll get in trouble. If I take something that doesn't belong to me, I'll be ashamed when someone finds what I took. People who do the wrong thing run away, and they don't know how to stop running. But when I'm right with You, I'm like a tree with strong roots that grow deep. I am solid, and I don't have to run away or be afraid. When I make wrong choices and break Your law, help me admit that You're right and I did the wrong thing. This helps me stop running and allows me to stay close to You.

BRAVE THINKING:

Why do people run from God
when they do the wrong thing?

⇒ FACING TROUBLE ⇐

The little troubles we suffer now for a short time are making us ready for the great things God is going to give us forever. We do not look at the things that can be seen. We look at the things that cannot be seen. The things that can be seen will come to an end. But the things that cannot be seen will last forever.
2 Corinthians 4:17–18

Dear God, brave boys face trouble, but it only lasts a short time. You have something better for me. I just need to wait. I can give my attention to all kinds of things, but many of those things never last. You, however, have asked me to give my attention to other things that will last forever. And it's those things that will outlast trouble. Those things get me ready to meet You. Those things will be proof that You have always loved me.

BRAVE THINKING:

What is the good news about facing trouble?

⤜ A COMPLETE STORY ⤛

*Learn well how to wait so you will be strong
and complete and in need of nothing.*

JAMES 1:4

Father, a tadpole has to wait to become a frog. A caterpillar has to wait to become a butterfly. I have to wait to become an adult. But I also have to wait to grow from being someone who is new to following You to one who is strong because You make me strong. It's no fun to wait, but I can learn while I wait. Give me a hunger for Your teaching. Give me a mind that understands it and a heart that will become wise as You teach. Help me remember that waiting for You means there is something special at the end of the waiting. Help me spend my life walking with You to a place where I'm strong and have a complete story filled with Your faithfulness and my obedience.

BRAVE THINKING:

What are some benefits of waiting?

⋟ I HAVE NEW LIFE ⋞

If then you have been raised with Christ,
keep looking for the good things of heaven.

COLOSSIANS 3:1

Dear God, Jesus died on the cross and then came back to life. That's good news for people like me who follow You, because it gives purpose to my life. I made the choice to give up my old life for the new life You have for me. That's good news for someone like me, because what You can give me is so much better than what I left behind when I started to follow You. Giving up my old life took courage because my old life was all I knew. It seemed hard to believe that I could learn to live a new way, but You loved me enough to teach and I loved You enough to learn—and You did give me new life and an amazing future.

BRAVE THINKING:

What do you want most from a new life in Christ?

THE EVERYDAY WALK AND TALK

So give yourselves to God. Stand against the devil and he will run away from you.

JAMES 4:7

Father, my gift to You is me. That's the one thing I can give You that You've always wanted. And even though I give myself to You, I got a gift back that's better than I could have imagined. You gave me a new life that is changing me and is noticed by others. Your enemy the devil tries to tell me that my old life was better. Help me to be brave enough to refuse to walk back the way I came. If I keep following You, then he has no interest in sticking around because he won't walk toward You. I have given myself to You, and You are my God. I want to walk with You today, talk with You today, and learn from You every day of my life.

BRAVE THINKING:

What is the one gift God wants from you? Does He have it yet?

⇒ THE BRAVE WORSHIP ⇐

*God is the One Who makes our faith
and your faith strong in Christ.*

2 CORINTHIANS 1:21

Dear God, I want to say words that worship You. What I could never do on my own is exactly what You do without any help. You made my faith strong when all I knew was weakness. When I couldn't understand the words in Your Book, You helped me understand them. When I wanted to run, You asked me to run to You. I'm strong because You gave me strength. I'm brave because You fight for me. I'm courageous because You've given me some incredible gifts. You give me hope and teach me to trust. You give me life, and You teach me to use it well. You give me peace, and I can refuse to worry. You stay with me. You make me brave.

BRAVE THINKING:

Why should God be honored
for making You brave?

SCRIPTURE INDEX

OLD TESTAMENT

MORE ENCOURAGEMENT AND WISDOM FOR BRAVE BOYS LIKE YOU!

100 Adventurous Stories for Brave Boys

Boys are history makers! And this deeply compelling storybook proves it! This collection of 100 adventurous stories of Christian men—from the Bible, history, and today—will empower you to know and understand how men of great character have made an impact in the world and how much smaller our faith (and the biblical record) would be without them.

Hardback / 978-1-64352-356-9 / $16.99